The Cato Institute

The Cato Institute is named for the libertarian pamphlets *Cato's Letters*, which were inspired by the Roman Stoic Cato the Younger. Written by John Trenchard and Thomas Gordon, *Cato's Letters* were widely read in the American colonies in the early eighteenth century and played a major role in laying the philosophical foundation for the revolution that followed.

The erosion of civil and economic liberties in the modern world has occurred in concert with a widening array of social problems. These disturbing developments have resulted from a major failure to examine social problems in terms of the fundamental principles of human dignity, economic welfare, and justice.

The Cato Institute aims to broaden public policy debate by sponsoring programs designed to assist both the scholar and the concerned layperson in analyzing questions of political economy.

The programs of the Cato Institute include the sponsorship and publication of basic research in social philosophy and public policy; publication of major journals on the scholarship of liberty and commentary on political affairs; production of debate forums for radio; and organization of an extensive program of symposia, seminars, and conferences.

Economic Forecasting–
Models or Markets?

Economic Forecasting– Models or Markets?

James B. Ramsey

With a Foreword by Murray N. Rothbard

CATO PAPER No. 10

CATO INSTITUTE
San Francisco, California

Reprinted by permission of the copyright holder, The Institute of Economic Affairs, London, © 1977.

Library of Congress Cataloging in Publication Data

Ramsey, James Bernard.
    Economic forecasting.

    (Cato paper ; no. 15)
    Bibliography: p.
    1. Economic forecasting. 2. Econometrics. 3. Micro-
economics. I. Title. II. Series.
HB3730.R33 1980   338.5'442   80-21911
ISBN-0-923790-28-3

Printed in the United States of America

CATO INSTITUTE
747 Front Street
San Francisco, California 94111

CONTENTS

FOREWORD

Economic forecasting has become a large and highly lucrative business. High-speed computers, using the most up-to-date and sophisticated econometric models, churn out predictions that are snapped up by a public hungry for the latest key to the future. And yet, for all its sophistication, econometric sooth-saying has been a string of failures. As Professor Ramsey points out in this essay, anyone, using only pencil and paper, can predict successfully, so long as current trends continue. It is the significant changes and turning points that are difficult to predict, and it is precisely at these points that econometric fore-casts have come a cropper. None of the sophisticated models, for example, was able to predict the double-digit inflation of 1973–74, or the beginning or intensity of the 1980 recession. Victor Zarnowitz, in a National Bureau study two decades ago, pointed out that the most sophisticated models did less well at forecasting than the most naive extrapolations of trend; and the story today is no different.

Professor Ramsey's essay is a useful critique of macroeco-nomic forecasting, of macroeconomics itself, and of the fail-ures of government intervention in the economy. Yet, at bot-tom, Professor Ramsey is still an econometrician, anxious to salvage the prestige of econometrics and save its reputation from the errors of the "untrained"; he therefore fails to pene-trate to the root of the problem. For while "naive" prediction deserves Ramsey's strictures, econometric models have fared no better. It is an open secret that the model builders, to make any sense of their results, have to fudge them with their own in-tuitive hunches.

The grave flaw lies at the heart of econometrics itself. Pro-fessor Ramsey persists in believing that the statement that "the quantity of a good demanded will fall when the price rises" is vague, loose, and imprecise, and that precision and sound theory only appear when the econometrician puts numbers, i.e., "coefficients," to this law and is able to say *how much* quantity purchased will fall when price rises by a certain amount. Such precision can only be illusory. *There are no constant numerical relations in human action*, and therefore there are no coefficients that can be included in this law that are not simply arbitrary and erroneous. Economic theory is and can only be qualitative—not quantitative. The vain quest for quantitative law has led to the dead ends of macroeconomics and economic forecasting that Ramsey reveals to us. It is simply the nature of human action, in contrast to that of natural phenomena, that its laws are only qualitative. At the root of the difference is the basic philosophical fact that human beings *choose*, that they adopt values and employ means to try to attain them, and that their values and chosen paths change all the time. These changes cannot be predicted, since human beings possess freedom of will and freedom of choice. Atoms, molecules, stones, etc., of course do not have free will, and do not make choices; so their behavior can be charted with quantitative and determinate precision.

Professor Ramsey tries to sidestep this difference by bringing in the magic of the stochastic. Human action and natural phenomena are the same: Both are probabilistic rather than precisely determined. Thus, the "science" of economics as a quantitative discipline can be salvaged, except that now the forecaster speaks of odds and probabilities rather than of spuriously precise numbers. The problem here is that for probability calculations to apply, certain crucial conditions must be met. In particular, the events subject to probability must be "homogeneous," that is, they must be identical to one another, and they must be "random," that is, each event must be totally unrelated to every other. There must be no causal chain linking the events.

Probability does enter into a few areas of human action, but these are minor and trivial. One example is a lottery; another is the playing of dice. The same dice are thrown throughout, and each throw of the dice is a separate event, independent of the other throws (unless the dice or the players are crooked). In that situation, we are able to say that, given a very large number of random throws, the number of times a one-spot will appear will tend to be one-sixth of the total number of throws (times the number of dice per throw); we can say that "the probability of the one-spot appearing on a die is one-sixth."

The application of probability analysis to human affairs, however, is strictly limited. It only works with chance events, random and homogeneous—a lottery, or even disease, deaths, or incidence of fire; in such areas insurance becomes economically practicable (except, of course, if the fires are not random and are set deliberately to collect the insurance). But stochastic analysis is *not* applicable to political or economic affairs. When a steel manufacturer is deciding whether or not to expand his plant, he must estimate what his future costs and revenues, and therefore his profits, will be. He is not faced with a very large number of homogeneous, random situations. On the contrary, each situation, each facet of the market that he faces, is unique and unrepeatable—though similar in many ways to other situations—and is linked in numerous causal ways to each other event. Nothing in human affairs or in the market economy is truly random; everything is linked and interwoven. And so the probability calculus is peculiarly inappropriate to economic affairs. Contrary to Professor Ramsey's notion, it is impossible to say what the odds are on any future economic event; there are no odds. Each event is unique, unrepeatable, and nonrandom. The probability calculus does not introduce welcome sophistication into economic theory and prediction; it only introduces grave and systemic error, and has led precisely to the sorry state of economic forecasting that Ramsey himself deplores.

Ralph Harris gets the matter right in his excellent supplement to Ramsey's book. As Harris points out, following Frank Knight's crucial distinction, the world of economic affairs is marked by pervasive *uncertainty,* which, in contrast to the measurable probabilistic world of "risk" (lotteries, roulette, etc.), cannot be scientifically forecast. Forecasting on the market is the function of the entrepreneur, and entrepreneurship in the final analysis is an art rather than a science, a matter of intuition, "hunch," and deep insight into the slice of the market that the entrepreneur knows and is dealing with. Successful entrepreneur-forecasters reap profits, and the unsuccessful absorb losses; so there is a long-run tendency in the market to

reward good forecasters and make them more important on the
business scene, and to punish the less competent forecasters
and drive them out of the ranks of entrepreneurs. Since it is an
art, entrepreneurship cannot be learned from textbooks or by
rote. As in the case of all creative or artistic talent, it cannot be
analyzed away; it can only be welcomed.

As Ludwig von Mises used to point out to those who were
tempted to succumb to the razzle-dazzle of economic forecasting: If someone were *really* able to forecast the economic
future, he wouldn't be wasting his time putting out market letters or econometric models. He'd be busy making several
trillion dollars forecasting the stock and commodity markets.
Let it be a reminder to anyone tempted to partake of, or give
credence to, this modern form of soothsaying.

August 1980   Murray N. Rothbard
                                                New York City

PREFACE
to the 1977 Edition

The *Hobart Papers* are intended to contribute a stream of authoritative, independent and lucid analysis to the understanding and application of economics to private and government activity. Their characteristic theme has been the optimum use of scarce resources and the extent to which it can best be achieved in markets within an appropriate framework of laws and institutions or, where markets cannot work or have disproportionate defects, by better methods with relative advantages or less decisive defects. Since the alternative to the market is in practice the state, and both are imperfect, the choice between them is essentially made on the judgment of "market failure" or "government failure."

The study of markets went through a period of decline after the war partly because of the ascendancy of Keynesian economics and its emphasis on macro quantities such as national output, expenditure, investment, and partly because of the emphasis on supposed "market failure," in turn arising from concern about the social costs and benefits, or "externalities," of the market processes of buying and selling. In recent years, Keynesian thinking has encountered increasing criticism; and externalities have been seen as not necessarily a source of market failure but as the result of inappropriate definition and enforcement of property rights. A third reason for the earlier decline of interest in markets has been the development of mathematical economics and the increasing use of econometrics in economic theory and applications to policy, in particular the use of economic "models" in attempts at forecasting. This third development is the subject of Professor James B. Ramsey's *Hobart Paper*.

IEA Papers have been concerned with macroeconomic models since the early years. In 1964 Dr. Malcolm Fisher of

Cambridge discussed their strengths and weaknesses[1] and in 1970 Professor Erich Streissler of the University of Vienna analyzed their "pitfalls."[2] In 1973 Professor L. M. Lachmann wrote a critique of macroeconomic thinking on the ground that it neglected the microeconomic foundations of the models used in economics.[3] He wrote as a theoretical economist associated with the Austrian school of economics. In 1974 Professor Mark Blaug wrote a critical analysis of macroeconomic theories of value and distribution, particularly as taught in the University of Cambridge (Great Britain) and reaffirmed the validity of the fundamental concepts of neoclassical micro theory.[4] In Hobart Paper 74 Professor Ramsey writes as an econometrician of the misuse or abuse of macroeconomic models by economists who have lost sight of their microeconomic components.

Professor Ramsey discusses what seem to be forbidding concepts and explains them in terms of everyday experience familiar in the life of the man in the street. He explains what economists can properly try to do, where economists who use macro methods have gone wrong, how they can put themselves right, and what useful purposes econometric methods can serve. He describes in remarkably simple language the difference between what are colloquially called "sure things" and "the odds" on an event taking place, or what the mathematical economist, in his forbidding jargon, calls deterministic and stochastic relationships. Economic laws are too often put into oversimple terms which suggest that a cause will be followed by a consequence without indication of the odds or chances that the consequence will take place. And it is here that econometrics can come to the rescue by refining vague economic generalities into quantitative economic indications.

Yet Professor Ramsey argues that economists who use models in attempts to foresee the consequences of given causes

[1] *Macro-Economic Models: Nature, Purpose and Limitations* (London: Institute of Economic Affairs, Eaton Paper 2).

[2] *Pitfalls in Econometric Forecasting* (London: IEA, Research Monograph 23).

[3] *Macro-Economic Thinking and the Market Economy* (London: IEA, Hobart Paper 56).

[4] The Cambridge Revolution: Success or Failure? (London: IEA, Hobart Paper 6, 1975).

and offer forecasts of events to come have not always been sufficiently careful or scientific. He claims that they have used
naïve models and ad hoc rules of thumb and have offered forecasts with insufficient economic justification.

Not least Professor Ramsey argues that uncritical adoption
of macroeconomic models and ways of thought have led economists to propose policies requiring central direction of economic activity that have had the most disappointing, if not dis-
astrous, results. And his exposition comes full circle when he
concludes his analysis by returning to the underlying requirement for the rational uses of resources: adjusting the framework of laws and institutions, notably those of property rights,
in order to make the all important micro relationships of individuals or individual firms in the market work to the satisfac-
tion of the general consumer's interest.

Professor Ramsey has, in his *Paper,* admirably explained
what seem to be difficult concepts for the reader with no
knowledge of economic theory. The reader will find a good
deal of enlightenment and stimulus in the text. There are several aspects of unusual interest to the lay reader as well as to the
student and the practitioner of economics. The use by forecasting organizations of naïve forecasting techniques embodying a
large element of subjective judgment, although occasionally
modified by semieconometric procedures, may have increased
because they are selling a service of quick but "dirty" forecasts
to government and industry which responds to the short-run
imperative of meeting deadlines and providing short-run
"predictions" that will seem "reasonable" to "practical"
men. Here Professor Ramsey is hinting that, in order to obtain
a favorable hearing for the indications of forecasting, the forecasters may be impelled to emphasize the more "politically
possible" or "administratively practicable" indications and to
understate those that politicians would find unpalatable and industry inconvenient.

Again, the production of forecasts for government and industry (and more recently trade unions and other organizations) demonstrates that there are both private and public
aspects of macro models. The "private" aspect is that the forecasters may be providing the best service they can, given the
short-term requirements of their clients. The "public" aspect is

that the models and their results are vulnerable on the ground of their deficient scientific bases and use. Moreover, the neglect of the microeconomic foundations is more acute in Britain than in the United States. This, says Professor Ramsey who has taught in and has links with both, may explain why the use of microeconomists in Britain is less than in the United States, where they are more aware of the limitations of models.

British readers accustomed to the neurotic pulse-taking of politicians and pundits will understand Professor Ramsey's criticism of the pressure by government for almost immediate information on the basis of flimsy stochastic ("odds on or against") evidence and their almost paranoic concern over small changes in published statistics from month to month, quarter to quarter, or even year to year. These changes are often smaller than the statistical error in the calculations, which are corrected not long after, so that the anxiety of politicians to draw the best conclusions from hustled, erroneous statistics is apt to make them look foolish. Perhaps most important, Professor Ramsey shows that, when the millions of decision makers and "forecasters" in the market are replaced by one governmental decision maker informed by one forecaster (or two, if the NIESR is regarded as an outside check on the Treasury), the result is instability in policy with largely unpredictable because politically motivated fluctuations. Far, therefore, from the market being the source of instability, events based on market decisions move much more slowly, predictably, and continuously than the lumpy jumps in economic events based on the destabilizing decisions of government.

To complement Professor Ramsey's analysis, Mr. Ralph Harris has written a short critique of forecasting models as used in Britain by the Treasury, the NIESR, and similar practitioners in the arts of foretelling the future. In his critique, based on a talk he gave to a gathering of civil servants, Mr. Harris questions the economic foundations of the models and the claims made for them as guides to central economic management. Here he develops the assessment of these models made by the late Mr. George Polanyi in 1973 in *Short-term Forecasting: a case study.*[5] He questions whether the knowl-

[5]IEA Background Memorandum 4, 1973.

edge required for forecasting by models is available; he maintains they reflect a confusion between corporate forecasting by individual firms and national planning by political governments; he illustrates his doubts by reference to centralized forecasting that has gone badly awry in Britain since the war; and he discusses the false "scientism" unavoidably embedded in the thinking on which macro models are based. He does not assert that the knowledge required for models can never be assembled by computer but that, until the knowledge is assembled, the models are a defective guide to policy and that markets, despite their imperfections—which are often government-created—are the best mechanism available to mankind.

We have to thank Mr. Richard Jackman of the London School of Economics and Professor Michael Parkin, late of the University of Manchester, now at the University of Western Ontario, Canada, for reading an early draft of Professor Ramsey's text and Professor Ivor F. Pearce for reading a draft of Mr. Harris's lecture and offering comments that both have taken into account in their final revisions. Its constitution requires the institute to dissociate its trustees, directors, and advisers from the analyses and conclusions of its authors but it offers Professor Ramsey's *Hobart Paper* as an authoritative and sophisticated, yet clearly and persuasively argued, analysis of the methods used in modern economics that will enlighten the student of economics and the noneconomist in industry and public life so that they will better judge the claims made for economic forecasting.

March–July 1977   Arthur Seldon

1. Introduction

Economics is the academic discipline most discussed by the general public. It is also one of the least understood. The press, radio, and television contain daily doses of "economic statistics" and even more injections of "economic comment" by everyone—except, by and large, economists.

Policy makers are unanimous that economics is vital. Yet they also largely seem to think that the less economists are consulted the better. This provocative observation requires some explanation, at least to the economist who frequently wonders why no one listens.

The prevailing confusion in economic matters is illustrated by a pair of quotations, which could easily have appeared in a British newspaper:

> When *laissez-faire* zealots object that planning will infallibly get us into a mess, one can only comment that it is hard to imagine a greater mess than the refusal to plan has got us into already: the worst inflation in a generation, the highest unemployment in 35 years, the worst decline in real output in nearly 40 years, the worst deficit in the balance of payments ever, the worst peacetime budgetary deficits ever, the worst energy shortages ever, the worst crisis in municipal finance ever.
>
> PROFESSOR ARTHUR SCHLESINGER, JR.,
> former adviser to President Kennedy,
> *Wall Street Journal,* July 30, 1975

> Surely Mr Schlesinger cannot believe that the market-place caused inflation or that it alone could control it; it is . . . government planners who caused inflation through excessive spending and expanding money supply. Few businessmen, straining as we all are to meet government standards, edicts, guidelines, and codes, would agree that the market-place is unregulated. Ours is a mixed econo-

my, but the government planners do not acknowledge the part their remedies of regulation have played in worsening our economic ills. Instead, ... the prescription is to increase the dosage....

T. A. MURPHY, Chairman,
General Motors Corporation,
Wall Street Journal, August 18, 1975

Each party to the dispute passionately believes he is right. Each will be able to cite statistics. But those of us who have lived through these arguments many times know that few will be persuaded, least of all the main disputants.

Why? Is it because economic arguments are merely about opinions and no one can really be right or wrong? Is an economist's opinion worth no more than anyone else's?

The economic dice

I will try in this paper to shed some light on these issues, to show what economic theory can and cannot achieve. I will indicate the role of econometrics in all this controversy—a mysterious word to some, pretentious to others, but important for the man in the street because economists using econometrics are influencing politicians in policies that very much affect his livelihood, standard of living, and way of life.

The paper begins by explaining the crucial role played by *chance* in economic events; it shows *we must learn how to bet on the economic dice* (section 2). Next it shows how econometric procedures are used to refine economic theory and enable economics to be called a science (section 3). These preliminaries set the stage for the discussion of forecasts and the use of economics in policy (section 4). Finally, it shows that the severe limitations to fiscal and monetary policy are more than compensated by the breathtaking scope of microeconomics, the economic theory of individual behavior (section 5). The paper ends (section 6) with a brief summary of the discussion which is illustrated by an eclectic review of a few of the major lessons practical experience has taught economists over the last twenty-five years.

2. The "Odds" in Economic Life Are More Common than the "Sure Thing"

I shall be using two technical terms that sound rather forbidding but have very familiar, even homely, meanings. The first, "deterministic," indicates a result with a definite fixed, single *point*—like a forecast that on a given day unemployment will be 5 percent of the labor force. The second, "stochastic," indicates that the result will be within a *range* of figures, with higher chances that it will lie near a central figure and lower chances that it will lie nearer the edges of the range. In other words, in everyday language, "deterministic" is used to indicate "a sure thing" and "stochastic" to indicate the "odds on (or against)" a result. We cannot say for sure which horse will win a race, but we can know the odds on any one horse winning. We cannot say what the unemployment percentage will be, but we can say that the odds against the percentage being below, say, 4 percent are 20 to 1.

We can all grasp what economists call "deterministic relationships" in real life, where the value of a "dependent variable" is "determined" (predicted) by the value of other "variables": For example, the temperature of a pint of water (dependent variable) depends upon, or is determined by, the original temperature of the water, its volume and pressure, and the amount of heat it receives. By specifying the values taken by the variables—volume, pressure, etc.—we can determine or predict—as a "sure thing"—the new temperature of the water. If the relationship between the rate of increase in the money supply and inflation were deterministic, we could say that an increase in prices (dependent variable) is determined by the amount of unemployment and the rate of increase in the money supply. Further, if the relationship were deterministic, we could predict as a sure thing the rate of inflation by specifying the values taken by the variables—unemployment, rate of increase in money supply.

"Stochastic relationships" are unknown in everyday language but are very common in everyday life. They involve "random variables," like the throw of dice, or drawing a card, or a horse race. In these relationships we cannot determine or predict the value of a dependent variable but we can say something about the probabilities or *chances* that it will fall within a *range*. Take an example from the real-life world of genetics. Suppose the dependent variable is the number of black and white mice in a litter and the other "variables" are factors in the genetic heritage of the parents. If we have information about the parents, we can say something about the expected proportion of black mice, or the probabilities of getting one or more black mice in a litter. In any *one* mating (in formal statistical language a "trial") there may be anything between all-black and all-white mice in the litter, but "on average," that is, if we were to observe a *large number* of matings and calculate the proportion of black mice, we would get an average ratio of say three out of five: We could say that the probability or chance of getting a black mouse is three out of five. In the more familiar language of sport or politics, an alternative method of expressing the random nature of the number of black mice in a litter is to talk about the "odds in favor or against,"[1] as in horse- and dog-races and general elections; e.g., that the odds in favor of two black mice in a litter of five are 2:3, or in favor of Labour winning in 1977/78 are, say, 60–40.

In economic predictions, we must always speak in terms of the odds for or against. The economist's statements are like: If the price of coffee increases by 20 percent, the odds in favor of an increase in the price of tea by at least 10 percent are 10:1; or, if the government imposes an interest-rate ceiling of 10 percent per annum, the odds against any increase in Building Society funds is 10,000:1.

Another way of expressing probability is to say that, although we do not know what will happen in a single mating or "trial," we do know what will happen in a very large number. Actuaries

---

[1] The relationship between the odds in favor of an event (say, three black mice) and probability is that the odds in favor equal the probability of the event occurring divided by the probability that it does not. If the probability of raining tomorrow is 3/5 and of not raining is 2/5, then the odds in favor of rain are 3:2.

cannot say how long you, the reader, will live, but they can state with considerable confidence how many readers out of ten thousand will survive to seventy. Probability is a formal way of expressing the proportion of times a given event (say, finding oil or natural gas) will occur in a large number of trials, or experiments, such as oil exploration drilling. An insurance company cannot predict whether your house will burn down, but they can determine the *probability* of your house burning down. And with this information they can calculate the insurance premium they must charge *you* in order to cover the risk of *your* house burning down. Similarly, an economist cannot predict whether your oil well *will* hit oil, but he can determine the *probability* of your well finding oil. And with this information he can calculate what the right to drill an oil well is worth to you.

What determines whether you live long or your house burns down?—conditioning variables

Important concepts in calculating probabilities and using them to predict events and make decisions are conditioning variables and conditional probabilities. The probability of an event, say your house burning down, depends upon the circumstances under which the trial or experiment is performed. These circumstances are called "conditioning" variables, in this case whether your house is heated electrically or by gas, whether you store old newspapers by the cooker, and so on. The probability of your surviving to sixty-five depends on whether you are in good health, your family has a history of heart trouble, and so on. The probability of drawing an ace from a pack of shuffled cards depends on how many cards, including aces, have already been dealt (the conditional probability would lie between one and zero—it is one if an ace is the only card left, zero if all four aces have been dealt, and one chance in thirteen if we are drawing the first card). The probability that house prices will rise next year in Birmingham depends on a very large number of conditioning variables: the net rate of migration into Birmingham, the supply of building land, governmental policies, and so on. In each case, the probabilities referred to are conditional probabilities because they depend upon, are determined by, the conditioning variables.

Life, based on chance, can be foreseen only as chances

Economic relationships are stochastic, not deterministic. An economist must express his predictions in the form of "odds": He says, if governmental policy and international trade conditions remain constant (the conditioning variables) there is only one chance in ten (the conditional probability) that the unemployment rate will fall below 3 percent. If economic relationships were deterministic, which they cannot be in a world of uncertainty, economists would be able to say that the unemployment rate would or would not fall below 3 percent. Unfortunately there are economists who say this, and they are fooling politicians (and you) and bringing economics into disrepute. Statements that next year, the gross domestic product (GDP) will be £109.640 billion, or that manufacturing employment will be 7.347 million persons, or that the money supply will be £19.260 billion, mislead in the extreme the reader who accepts such numbers with all their apparent but spurious decimalized accuracy. What can be said is that if the assumptions underlying these estimates hold, that is, if the values of the conditioning variables do not change, the probability that GDP will be in the range £109 to £111 billion is .9 and the probability of GDP being more than £111 billion is 0.05. Similar probability statements can be made about the other variables.

The reader, I am sure, will agree that trying to understand such statements about probabilities of GDP lying in some range is much harder than understanding the simple statement "GDP will be..."; but the probability statement is at least honest. And, once you understand the ideas involved, the probability statements are not much harder to grasp.

An immediate benefit of such knowledge is that a newspaper report like "Preliminary figures indicate that last quarter the consumer price index rose by 0.5 percent" will now receive the yawn it deserves instead of the barrage of political accusations and counteraccusations it would now stimulate. For even supposedly recorded figures, such as price indices, unemployment statistics, and so on are no more than "random"; that is, there is some probability that the true, but unknown, figure is more than the cited figure and some probability that it is less. To continue our price index example, the probability that the "increase" was in fact a *decrease* as low as 1 percent might be as probable as that the increase was as high as 1 percent. Finally, when you observe that the "revision of preliminary estimates" of such indices often involves much larger changes than 0.5 percent, your faith in such evanescent figures evaporates rapidly.

Almost all scientific disciplines have been moving in recent years from deterministic to stochastic formulations of their theories. Genetics is a stochastic science since genetic relationships depend upon conditional probabilities. High energy physics is a stochastic science because atoms behave randomly: A physicist cannot prescribe the path of a *single* atom but can say something about the behavior of large *numbers* of atoms. Engineering is a stochastic science because machines break down randomly, the quality of materials varies randomly from one batch to another, and so on. *The more precise and detailed we try to make our theories, the more we have to express them stochastically.* If we merely wish to say that a spring "will extend" if a weight is added, that idea can be stated deterministically. But if we want to say *how much* it will extend by adding a 50-gram weight, the idea must be expressed stochastically. If a scientist repeats an experiment of adding weights on to a spring, he will get different lengths of extension, and will therefore be able to describe his results in terms of probabilities. Economics, far from bringing up the rear of these efforts to refine relationships, has been in the vanguard.

Testing "sure things" and "odds on (or against)"

The testing of "sure thing" deterministic relationships is relatively easy to understand. If the hypothetical statement is that, say, an increase in heat (the conditioning variable) raises the temperature (the dependent variable) of an object, and if we heat an object but the temperature does not rise, the statement has been "tested"; in this case it must be rejected as an inaccurate description of reality.

With "odds on (or against)" (stochastic) formulations, testing is not so simple. For a start, the hypothetical statements are not in the simple form of: "If A, then B." The simplest statements might be in the form: "If the supply of money is increased by 20 percent in six months, the probability that the rise in prices will exceed 25 percent or be below 15 percent in eighteen to twenty-four months is one chance in five thousand.'' Thus, if the formulation of a hypothetical statement is put in terms of the conditional *probabilities* of occurrence of events, ''testing'' the theory involves checking probabilities. We have to calculate from a large number of experiments the *probability* of the event and compare it with the prediction.

The testing of ''odds'' (stochastic) relationships is thus considerably more complex and requires much more data. A predicted relationship cannot be rejected on the basis of a single trial, but only after a period of time with the accumulation of evidence against it. When, on the basis of the evidence, the probability of the statement being consistent with the observed data is small, say, less than one chance in one thousand, we may reasonably conclude that the statement has been rejected by the evidence. In other words, we can then say that the statement is not a useful, or accurate, description of reality because it does not predict.

This distinction between ''sure thing'' and ''odds on (or against)'' relationships is somewhat exaggerated. In practice, the use and testing of almost all hypothesized relationships must be couched in terms of odds, if for no other reason than to take account of errors of measurement made in observing an event. For example, if ten people try to measure accurately the rise in the cost of living, they will obtain ten different numbers. The same problem arises with most statistics. Errors arise due both to errors made by the observer and to imperfections in the measuring instruments.

These arguments are most important in discussing macroeconomics, the economic theory of national income, total consumption by everyone, national levels of investment, etc. Since economics is a stochastic science, and macroeconomic variables are observed with error, sometimes large, predictions about the economy can be put only in terms of conditional probabilities, not of the definite occurrence of particular events. Forecasts of macroeconomic quantities such as national expenditure on consumption or investment, or national average incomes or prices, or exports or imports, should be in the form that, if government expenditures and the money supply remain constant, the conditional probability that the gross domestic product will be less than £110 billion is one chance in a hundred; or that the conditional probability that unemployment will be less than 4 percent or more than 5 percent is five chances in a thousand. Unfortunately such macroeconomic forecasts by government (or private) economists are rarely put in this form but in the more impressive but spurious form of single figures.

The conditioning variables underlying the forecast must be clearly indicated if the prediction is to be understood. It is vitally important for the general understanding of economic pronouncements to stress the conditional and probabilistic nature of macroeconomic forecasts. Thus, if the money supply were to increase, in the above example, the current forecasts of gross domestic product and unemployment are no longer correct statements. The new statement might be that with an extra 5 percent increase in money supply, the probability that gross domestic product will be more than £112 billion is one chance in a hundred, and that the probability of unemployment being more than 5 percent is now only one chance in a thousand.

With these preliminaries completed, we can now discuss the roles of econometrics and show how to interpret economic predictions and forecasts.

3. Econometrics: The Bridge between Theory and Real Life

The masthead to *Econometrica,* a journal of econometrics, states that econometrics is concerned with "the advancement of economic theory in its relation to statistics and mathematics." In the sense of the application of statistical methods in measuring economic variables, econometrics has a venerable history almost as old as economics itself; an early example is Sir William Petty's *Political Arithmetik* published in 1690. Two dates—1930, when the Econometrics Society was formed, and 1946, the beginning of the postwar period—mark major watersheds in the development of the discipline. Until 1930 econometrics was seldom concerned with little more than measuring a few economic variables, usually the prices and quantities of goods traded over a period. Occasionally attempts would be made to "test" economic relationships, i.e., to compare an economic prediction with actual events. Professor G. J. Stigler, for example, attributes the first "estimation" of a demand equation to Charles Davensant, who published his work in 1699.[1] This work can be regarded as a pioneer attempt to test the idea that an increase in price reduced the quantity demanded. But there were two major stumbling blocks to more extensive testing.

One was that the theory of statistics itself—the theory of how to relate ideas to events in a stochastic, not a deterministic, world—was incomplete. Another was that the ideas of "hypotheses," "theories," and their "tests" were understood only imperfectly. The methodology of scientific inference was in its infancy.

---

[1] *Essays in the History of Economics* (Chicago: University of Chicago Press, 1965), p. 213.

The formative years

Nineteen thirty marks the beginning of econometrics as we know it today. From then we can date the shift from a little measurement and scattered examples of casual testing of ideas toward the development of economics as a stochastic science, which must concern itself with random variables, chances of occurrence, and the "odds in favor of" (or against) events.

Nineteen forty-six marks the beginning of the postwar period during which time econometric "facts" or data were subtantially improved and the scope of the science extended. This is the period during which econometricians discovered how to identify the effect of a specific variable on another by using data generated not by carefully controlled experiments, but by the world itself, that is, by published statistics of national income, investment, consumption. In short, the econometrician had at last discovered a way of overcoming (sometimes at least) his age-old handicap of not being able to experiment. The advantage of the natural over the social scientist was narrowed significantly.

A related and crucially important development was the ability through computers to handle large numbers of variables which interact with one another in a very complex manner. For example, the numerous recent econometric studies on the demand for and supply of (natural) gas and petroleum in the United States would not have been physically possible even thirty years ago.[2]

By these developments yet another advantage of the natural scientist, his ability to control the environment of his experiment, was diminished. In both cases, the econometrician was able to compensate in some measure for his inability to experiment by developing more sophisticated statistical tools.

Econometrics is thus the bridge between theory and fact in two senses. First, it is the tool by which economic theory can be tested. And, second, it is essential in deciding economic policy.

[2]Only one example of many in the literature is: Professors E. A. Hudson and Dale W. Jorgenson, "US Energy Policy and Economic Growth, 1975-2000," *The Bell Journal of Economics and Management Science* 5, no. 2 (Autumn 1974): 161-514.

From sham to reality—econometrics and testing economic theory

The claim of economics to be a science must be based on its method. The scientific method is, very simply, the procedure by which ideas about how the world functions are continually tested, so that theory is confronted with reality. The more severe and challenging the test, the more we learn about our discipline, whether the idea under test is rejected or not. The short-run objective of every scientist is to try to refute the existing, or currently entertained, ideas; he tries to test and if possible reject the conventional wisdom. If he succeeds, we know we must find other explanations. If he fails, our confidence in the prevailing view is increased.

Consequently, the fundamental role of econometrics is to specify the procedures required to test economic ideas. There are several aspects. Given that economic occurrences are best described by stochastic relationships but that most conventional economic theory is put in deterministic form, the first task of econometrics is how to transform spurious deterministic "sure things" into realistic stochastic "odds." This is not easy but, until we can translate economic theory into a form which can be applied to what we observe in real life, it is merely an intellectual exercise with no useful relationship to the real world.

What is more fundamental to life than bread? Suppose the Able Bakery wants to know how much the demand for its bread will fall if it raises the price. If the price is increased by 5 percent, some customers may not change their consumption of Able's bread very much at all, others will stop buying it altogether, and the rest will change their consumption somewhere in between. The important question for Able Bakery is not whether there will be a decrease, but by *how much* demand will decrease. Further, it knows that, from week to week, bread sales vary "randomly," that is, one week it sells 1,000 loaves, the next week 950, the week after 1,045, the week after that 995, and so on, but that "on average" it sells 1,000 loaves a week at 20p a loaf. What it wants to know is: If the price of its bread is now 21p per loaf, how many loaves will it sell "on average"?

For the econometrician to bring economic theory to bear on this problem, he must express it in a form which takes into account the random variation in the sales of the Able Bakery's bread. The relevant formulation of economic theory must be able to cope with such statements as: If the price of bread is increased, average consumption will fall. Further, large sales of bread in any week (say, more than 1,100 loaves) will be more unlikely than before, e.g., before the price change the bakery expected to sell as much as 1,100 loaves only one week in ten (the probability is one in ten), now it expects to sell that much only one week in twenty (a probability of one in twenty). Small sales of bread, say, less than 900 loaves in a week, are now more likely. The conditional probabilities of selling various amounts of bread have been changed by a change in the conditioning variable, price.

A further problem is that while the Able Bakery is interested in the effect on demand of increasing the price, the econometrician is aware that many variables other than price affect quantity demanded, such as consumer incomes, the prices of other goods, family size, age distribution of the population, etc. If all these other variables are not going to change in the near future, and if all the Able Bakery is concerned about is the *change* in demand to a *change* in price, then the econometrician can ignore these other conditioning variables. But if it is known, for example, that the price of potatoes is going to fall very shortly, then the econometrician must allow for the resulting effect on the demand for bread. In the real world we seldom observe only one conditioning variable changing; the econometrician must therefore isolate the effects of each conditioning variable on the dependent variable. While the physical scientist is usually able to isolate the effects of each of his conditioning variables by the way in which he designs his experiments, the economist must use nature's own, and by no means optimally designed, experiments and rely on sophisticated statistical tools to disentangle the separate effects of each conditioning variable.

The reader may be aware of the claim that the physical sciences are experimental, but the social sciences are not. This is not the true distinction, for both are experimental; the advantage of the physical sciences is that they are more able to rely on experiments *controlled by the scientist himself,* not on "experiments" generated by others for wholly nonscientific reasons. Thus, no politician is likely to take seriously the notion of running a controlled experiment with variations in the money supply, even though evidence generated by it might settle a number of politically disputatious issues such as the relationship between interest rates and the rate of change of the money supply.[3]

A more difficult situation is where a conditioning variable that has not changed in the past is expected to change in the future. Trying to predict the dependent variable under these circumstances is often impossible. It poses the most formidable challenge to the econometrician's mastery of both economic theory and the procedures of scientific inference. If a scientist has always observed the relationship between heat and the temperature of boiling water at a given constant pressure, it is hard to predict the precise effect on the boiling temperature of water if the pressure is changed. Similarly, if the price of potatoes has not been observed to change, it is difficult to predict the precise effect on the demand for bread when it does change.

Loose (economic) laws and precise (econometric) results

Much "sure thing" deterministic economic theory leads to relations between variables which are too vague or general to permit rigorous testing and use of the theory. The econometrician tries to create a more refined result out of loose economic rules. It is not enough to say that if the price of a good rises, consumption will fall. We have to be more specific, or precise, about how much it falls. Does it fall proportionately to the rise in price? Does the extent of the fall depend on the level of the price before the change? Is consumption expected to fall immediately, or after a few weeks?

The econometrician has had to fill the gap between loose ideas and precisely stated hypotheses by recasting the hypothesized relationships in terms of a specific mathematically formulated model. Reformulation in mathematical form is necessary if hypotheses are to be tested with rigor. Consequently, the econometrician must thoroughly understand economic theory so that the specific formulations he creates are useful for

---

[3][Some socioeconomic experiments may be technically feasible, for example with a type of reverse income tax in New Jersey, a school voucher in California, and a housing voucher in Australia.—ED.]

testing economic conjectures. The analysis of the relationship between quantity demanded and price is an excellent example. The objective is not simply to write down any specific form of the relationship, i.e., any mathematically formulated model, but to specify a mathematical model which satisfies all the requirements of the theory. Current practice is in marked contrast to earlier efforts in which the mathematical models used to test economic theory violated at least some of the requirements of the theory. Such models obviously cannot provide a valid test of a theory. For example, models of the relationship between the quantity demanded and the price of a good (what economists call the demand equation) must satisfy an "adding-up criterion," that is, the sum of quantity demanded multiplied by the respective prices of all goods purchased must add up to the consumer's income. This adding-up criterion must be satisfied for any group of prices the consumer might face. Early models of demand equations often did not satisfy this criterion.

The formulation of a mathematical model of a hypothesis involves specifying the relationship between the variables of interest in terms of "coefficients." Essentially, each coefficient indicates the weight to be attached to the effect of a conditioning variable on the dependent variable. Different values given to the coefficients mean different weights attached to the effects of each of the conditioning variables. When the right numbers are substituted for the coefficients we can calculate, for example, that 40.1 tons of potatoes will be demanded if the price is £6.00 per ton and average consumer income is £400 per year. Another way to say this is, given information on the actual amounts of potatoes demanded, the price, and so on, we "solve" the abstract mathematical model which relates quantities of potatoes to price, etc., by assigning the required numbers to the coefficients. We assign the numbers so that, in our model relating potatoes to price, if we substitute the amount £6.00 for the price variable we get as "answer" 40.1 tons of potatoes. But, once the coefficient values are known, we can use them to answer such questions as "How many tons of potatoes will be demanded if the price is £5.00 per ton and the average income is £800 per year?"; or, ". . . if the price is £9.00 per ton and the average income is only £300 per year?"

Institutions affect the application of theory to real life

The pure theorist usually finds it convenient to ignore the details of existing institutions, such as banks, firms, laws of property rights, (laws which specify how and to what extent an individual can use his property), and so on, when developing theoretical ideas.[4] Econometricians, however, must have a sound knowledge of the institutional details, in addition to their theory, if they are to apply economic theory to real-life problems. Institutional knowledge is needed to formulate the models correctly, to incorporate various constraints imposed by the institutions, and to be able to evaluate the effects of possible changes in the institutional arrangements. Thus, the imposition of price ceilings will alter the way in which a market functions. The inability to sue for breach of contract introduces elements of risk and a larger need for market information into the analysis of supply and demand. The recent change in U.K. banking regulations altered the relationship between the commercial banks and the Bank of England and so the availability of credit.

Another aspect of this need for institutional knowledge is a thorough understanding of the way in which the data were collected and the extent to which they represent measurements of theoretical concepts. That a statistic is labeled "consumption" or "income" does not necessarily mean that the numbers measure what economists understand by these concepts. For example, a farmer's consumption of his own produce is part of his income, a salesman's use of his own firm's products is also part

[4]This statement is no longer strictly true. One of the most exciting developments in economic theory is the attention economists are once again paying to the analysis of institutional arrangements. Economists are now endeavoring to explain the reasons for differences in economic institutions and to explain the effects of such differences on economic behavior. For example, economists are analyzing the behavior of governments, agencies, and bureaucracies by modifying old tools of analysis and developing new ones. So-called nonprofit and charitable institutions are now under the economist's scalpel. The economic implications of labor-managed firms and the role of the firm in socialist economics are now receiving attention (B. Chiplin, J. Coyne, and L. Sirc, *Can Workers Manage?* (London: Institute of Economic Affairs, Hobart Paper 76, 1977). And finally, the entire process of drawing legal contracts is bringing together the economist and the legal expert. (If the reader pursues some of the titles listed in Recommended Reading at the end of this paper, he will receive an excellent introduction to this material.)

of his income, while neither is reflected in national income statistics. Statistically much more important is the exclusion from national income statistics of the contribution of housewives to real (as opposed to officially measured) national income. The very large amount of this contribution becomes apparent to the government official only when household activities are brought into the purview of the tax authorities, i.e., when a mother enters the officially recorded labor force and hires someone else to do the housework. In reality, all that has happened in such a transaction is that the housewife has changed jobs, but there has been an increase in national income only if and to the extent that she is more productive in the new job than the old. But the official statistics would record an increase in employment of two and an increase in national income equal to the sum of the two women's officially recorded incomes.

Disentangling cause and consequence

In the introduction to this section I indicated that the most important innovation by econometrics was the concept of identification—the procedure by which relationships between two variables can be isolated from complex relations among large numbers of variables. The need for "identification" arises because economists usually cannot experiment like the natural scientists.

Loosely stated, economic theory predicts that if the price of a good increases, the amount demanded will fall. Suppose you are given two sets of numbers: One is the price of wheat in England for various years during the nineteenth century; the other is the corresponding amounts of wheat sold at those prices. You discover, on looking at these figures, that in some years prices rose and the quantity sold fell; so far so good. But, on looking further, you see that in other years in which prices fell, the quantity fell as well; and in yet other years prices either fell or rose, but quantity sold did not change. Clearly, something is wrong. Should we reject the conjecture that an increase in price reduces quantity demanded? The answer is: not yet, for testing is not so easily accomplished. Let us reconsider our real-world-produced data.

Economic theory also predicts that if price rises the quantity supplied will rise. But our data are not consistent with this hypothesis either. However, economic theory predicts that, in the absence of constraints on trade arrangements such as price ceilings, trade will take place when quantity demanded equals quantity supplied; in technical terms mutual adjustment between supply, demand, and price will tend toward equilibrium. Therefore, what we have observed are prices and quantities *traded,* and the prices are those for which the quantity demanded equals the quantity supplied.[5] In fact, we have observed neither a demand relationship (or equation) nor a supply relationship (or equation). If this is all the information we have, we are in trouble, for there is no way of disentangling the demand equation from the supply equation in our mathematical model of this market.

Before we see how this apparently hopeless situation can be saved, let us consider what would have happened if someone had run an experiment. Suppose a nineteenth-century economist were given control over the entire wheat supply. We suppose he sets a price for wheat and records the amount demanded. The next year he repeats the experiment with a new price, and so on. Under these conditions[6] we will observe a demand equation, a relationship between quantity demanded and price. Alternatively, our experimenting economist could have set a price at which he was prepared to buy all wheat supplied and measured the amount supplied. In this way he would be able to observe the supply equation for nineteenth-century English wheat farmers.

Let us return to our econometric problem of trying to determine the relationship between quantity demanded and price. Economic theory predicts that the demand for wheat depends not only on price but also on the incomes of the consumers, the prices of other goods, and so on. Suppose we discover that, although we cannot obtain measurements on the variables affect-

[5]In terms of the mathematical model of the wheat market, there are two relationships (or equations), a supply equation and a demand equation. Market equilibrium, at which trade occurs, is expressed in terms of the model as the "solution to a pair of simultaneous equations," that is, the model determines the price at which quantity supplied equals quantity demanded.

[6]To keep the example simple and suppress unnecessary details, I am assuming that, while the experiment is being run, there is no change in population, in its income, in the prices of other goods, etc. In short, the other "conditioning variables" remain constant.

ing consumption other than income, we do have evidence that they remained unchanged over the relevant period. Thus, over this period we have two variables affecting quantity demanded: price and consumers' incomes.

Next, we examine conditions on the supply side of the market and discover that everything theory predicts would affect supply, except the weather, remained constant. Thus, we have only two variables affecting quantity supplied: price and the weather.

In this example, nature has been kind for we have a very simple situation involving only five variables (the quantity of wheat supplied and demanded, price of wheat, incomes, and the weather) and four sets of information or data, price of wheat, quantity of wheat traded, income, and the weather. Add to this the information that there were no obstacles to the market being in equilibrium in each period, so that quantity demanded equaled quantity supplied, and our problem is nearly solved. In the technical language, we say that the demand and supply relationships are "identified."

Now we can see more clearly the advantage of the natural (experimenting) scientist over the social (nonexperimenting) scientist. The major objective of the natural scientist in *designing* his experiment is to make sure that his observed relationships are identified. The economist has to discover whether "nature" performed an experiment with this desirable property. If so, all is well, but if not, there is nothing the economist can do; the available evidence cannot be used to test hypotheses about demand or supply, nor to make predictions about the effects of changes in price or income on the quantity of wheat traded. If the relationships are *not* "identified," *nothing* can be concluded from the evidence.

All that remains is the technical problem of assigning numbers to the unknown values of the "coefficients" in the mathematical model: the numbers which enable us to say that 995,643 bushels of wheat will be demanded if the price is 6 shillings a bushel and each consumer's income is £20 per year, or if the price rises to 6s 6d only 994,256 bushels of wheat will be demanded. In deterministic models assigning numbers to the coefficients is known as "solving the equations," and in stochastic models "estimation."

In our simple example, the demand equation was "identified," because we were able to combine economic theory with enough quantitative information to be able to relate quantity demanded to the price of wheat. If there had been *no* change in the weather and therefore *no* change in the amount of wheat supplied at all possible prices, we would not have been able to "identify" the demand equation; we would have been unable to predict how quantity demanded was related to price.

We see from this example that, because the amount of wheat traded in each year depended on consumer incomes and the weather as well as price, we could observe that with prices up, the quantity traded might be up, down, or unchanged. As a result of our efforts in identifying the demand equation, the "estimation" of our mathematical model enables us to predict the change in the quantity of wheat demanded to a change in incomes, the change in quantity supplied to a change in price, and the effect of weather on the production of wheat.

The parable of the Russian peasants

This brief discussion about the problem of identification—the problem of how to recognize a specific relation between a pair of variables within a complex set of variables—indicates that the task of relating theory to practice is fraught with many difficult and subtle traps for the unwary. Another aspect of this general problem is the question: When does an observation that two happenings tend to occur together imply that one *causes* the other? or merely *accompanies* it, possibly as consequences of a common cause? Consider this (apparently true) story:

> There was once a cholera epidemic in Russia. The government, in an effort to stem the disease, sent doctors to the worst-affected areas. The peasants of the province of S—— discussed the situation and observed a very high correlation between the number of doctors in a given area and the incidence of cholera in that area [i.e. more doctors were observed in cholera areas than elsewhere]. Relying on this hard fact, they rose and murdered their doctors.[7]

[7]Professor Franklin M. Fisher, *The Identification Problem in Econometrics* (New York: McGraw-Hill, 1966), pp. 2–3.

To us, perhaps, the Russian peasants acted foolishly. What they did was to form an idea about the joint occurrence of doctors and cholera, observe some evidence in support of the hypothesis, and then act in accordance with their incorrect (but as yet unrejected) idea. What might they have done which would have been more sensible? They should have tried to *test* their idea about the relationship of doctors and cholera by either observing more carefully that cholera arrived *before* the doctors, or by sending doctors into a cholera-free village and observing what happened.[8]

The purpose of this story is to show that if you observe two events occurring together, the association does not necessarily imply causality. The observed relationship may be due to chance —a random event; or it may be that both events are affected by some outside event. A continuous increase in the money supply, for example, will create inflation and raise the interest rate on bonds. The increase in the interest rate does not *cause* the inflation, even though high interest rates are *associated* with inflation.

Consider the relationship between investment and interest rate in the capital goods market, i.e., the demand for and supply of capital goods. The demand equation is the relation of the demand for capital goods (investment) to the interest rate. The supply equation is the relation between the supply of capital goods (equipment, buildings, etc.) and the price of capital goods. But both demand and supply equations depend on other variables in the economy besides the interest rate, so that a simple relationship between interest rate and investment is not likely to be observed. We may observe investment spending rising with higher interest rates, and vice versa, as well as apparently no relationship at all. The situation is entirely analogous to the example of nineteenth-century wheat. Some of the other variables which affect both the demand for and supply of investment goods, and which can prevent us from observing a simple relationship between investment demand and interest rate, are:

---

[8]The astute reader might at this point wonder whether politicians and those Russian peasants are really so different—both have taken drastic and precipitate action on the basis of casual observation and with no thought to testing the hypotheses used to justify their behavior.

expectations about future profits which in turn depend upon expectations about prices and costs, technological changes in the capital equipment industry, the exchange rate, domestic and foreign trade restrictions such as quotas and tariffs, and so on.

What this example illustrates primarily is that intuition and casual empiricism, far from being simple proxies for econometric analysis, can be grossly misleading. This idea is even more important when trying to relate current profit levels to current investment. Indeed, other than lowering the cost of borrowing for investment, current profits have little to do with current (as opposed to future) investment levels.

The short and the long (term) and the tall (story), or Why the general secretary of the Labour party went wrong

A letter to the *Times* from Mr. Ronald Hayward, the general secretary of the Labour party, illustrates the confusion:

> For the 12 months, fourth quarter 1971 to third quarter 1972, net company profits rose by 26.2 per cent. But investment in manufacturing fell by 2.3 per cent in cash terms and no less than 14.7 per cent in real terms... I think these figures illustrate my point that private investment is failing the nation.[9]

This quotation suggests that Mr. Hayward subscribes to the idea that an increase in current profits indicates a *permanent* increase in demand so that investment expenditures "ought" to be increased, even if businessmen generally do not take this view. Plainly, a current increase in profits does not necessarily indicate a permanent increase in demand. The increase could be due to a partial recovery from previous low profit levels and firms might still have excess capacity; an analysis of expected conditions may indicate that the current profit increase is temporary; or future conditions may be so uncertain that firms find it optimal to "wait and see." Extensive and sophisticated analysis would be needed before we could reasonably conclude either that firms were not maximizing profits by their behavior,

[9]R. G. Hayward, the (London) *Times,* February 26, 1973.

or, even if they were, that an increase in investment would be "socially desirable." For example, assuming that the lack of investment was consistent with profit maximizing behavior, a government-enforced increase in investment might lead to an increased rate of inflation, followed by excess capacity and idle resources, including labor. In short, government action based on the observed association of low investment with high profits could increase the severity of the business cycle, not diminish it. In effect, without knowing whether the relationship between investment and profit rates is identified, one cannot draw *any* valid conclusions from such evidence.

This quotation illustrates a further pernicious aspect of such casual observations as those of Mr. Hayward. He observed only *one* year; why not at least the whole post–World War II period, not to mention the entire statistical history of profits and investment? For example, in the post–World War II period alone, investment was up with profits up for the years 1949–51, '53–55, '57, '60, '61, '64, '65, '68, '70, '71, but investment was down with profits up for the years 1959, '62, '63, and, of course, '72, or investment was up with profits down for the years 1952, '56, '66, and '69, and so on. Clearly, the situation is entirely analogous to the wheat example. Mr. Hayward in this quotation engaged in the practice of citing only evidence which agreed with his claim and ignoring that which did not. When discussions about economic events are carried on in this fashion there can never be any resolution to the argument. This is why neither side in a politically motivated debate convinces the other. We now have part of the answer to the questions posed in the Introduction.

I hope this analysis demonstrates the potential harm to the economy of pursuing policies based on such a cursory examination of transitory evidence. What is astonishing is that, for many people and almost all politicians, such impressionistic statements, made in all quarters, are held to be superior to evidence obtained by applying a carefully formulated theory to *all* the available data over a period. One explanation, of course, is that the policy maker, unlike the scientist, is primarily interested in the data which support his hypothesis, not those which are inconsistent with it and hence which would cast doubt on the usefulness of his theory.

Galbraith's missing evidence

To illustrate the role of econometrics in testing hypothetical statements or ideas about how the world functions, let us take an example from Professor J. K. Galbraith's attacks on what he presents as "conventional economic wisdom" in *The New Industrial State.*[10] To the noneconomist (and even to many economists) he writes plausibly and entertainingly, but his ideas have been the subject of more public discussion than rigorous testing. Into this breach stepped Professor Harold Demsetz with an examination of Galbraith's assertions which provides a telling example of the role of econometrics in the testing of hypotheses.[11]

The first hurdle Professor Demsetz faced was that "Galbraith's lively prose seldom allows its author a clearly testable hypothesis."[12] In short, his immediate task was to reformulate Galbraithian notions in a form suitable for testing. First, "technostructure-oriented firms," said Galbraith, "sacrifice profits in order to accelerate growth of sales."[13] Second, such firms are able to achieve more stability in their operations because they can control prices and output through the monopoly control of their industries and by "creating" demand through advertising.

Professor Demsetz examined data on 375 industries in the United States for 1958 to 1970, the maximum period over which all the data were available. He considered three alternative measures of instability of operations and four alternative measures of the degree of "technostructure orientation." He also considered several alternative formulations of the two hypotheses. The result of Professor Demsetz's econometric

[10]Boston: Houghton Mifflin Co., 1967.

[11]Harold Demsetz, "Where is the New Industrial State?" *Economic Inquiry,* March 1974, pp. 1-12. Fortunately, there is usually someone willing to test our ideas and the best tests often come, not from the originator of an idea, but from other scientists. I do not think Professor Galbraith has ever rigorously tested his own ideas. The economic profession is in Professor Demsetz's debt.

[12]Ibid., p. 1.

[13]Ibid.: Technostructure-oriented firms are firms which utilize high levels of technology and high rates of expenditure on capital relative to labor, e.g., oil companies or IBM or ICI.

analysis is, in his own words:

> The only conclusion permitted by this investigation is that Galbraith's notions are remarkably consistent in their inability to find confirmation.[14]

Professor Demsetz is to be congratulated on a cryptic understatement of his results. I have never seen a pair of hypotheses rejected by the data so completely and so extensively.

---

[14]Demsetz, "Where is the New Industrial State?" p. 11.

4. Economic Forecasting versus Prediction — Science or Astrology?

An economic forecast, whether in micro- or macroeconomics, is really saying "what will happen *if* ..."

—What will happen to the supply of rented housing *if* a ceiling on rents is enforced?

—What will happen to the quantity and price of wheat traded *if* a new strain is introduced?

—What will happen to the interest rate *if* the money supply is increased?

—What will happen to the price of tea *if* the price of coffee increases?

Forecasts are by their nature "conditional": They depend on the circumstances surrounding the situation—the "conditioning events." The supply effect of a rent ceiling depends upon the existing conditions in the housing market. Is there excess housing capacity? What are the laws determining the property rights of landlords and renters? And so on. The effect of an increase in the money supply on interest rates depends on many other related variables in the economy: whether there is inflation; whether there are unemployed men and machines; the size of government expenditure; taxation policy; whether the exchange rate for the pound is fixed; foreign interest rates; expectations about future prices and interest rates, etc.

Secondly, economics as a stochastic science must concern itself with the *chances* of an event happening, the *odds* in favor or against, the *probability* of occurrence. The type of statements which can be made are: If current circumstances in the tea market remain unchanged (this statement summarizes the "conditioning events"), and if the government pursues a policy of noninterference in the tea market, the odds in favor of the price of tea rising by at least 2p per pound are 3:1 and odds against a price fall are 10:1.

This is an example of a forecast of the effect of a policy decision: In this case the decision is not to interfere. We also see from this example that a forecast has three important aspects: specification of the circumstances on which the forecast is based; application of a theory to the problem; statement of the result in terms of conditional probabilities, that is, giving the odds in favor assuming that the circumstances remain as stated. Forecasts are merely statements about the *probability* of a result occurring, and their usefulness depends upon the correctness of the theory used and upon the "accuracy" of the assumptions about the underlying circumstances. If the theory is wrong, that is, it would be rejected if tested, or does not apply to the given problem, the forecast is invalid; the statements about the odds in favor are incorrect. Secondly, if the assumed circumstances change, the forecast is invalid. For example, suppose we forecast that if there is a 5 percent increase in government expenditure, the odds in favor of a decrease in unemployment to 4 percent are 4:1, *assuming* all existing circumstances in the economy remain unchanged and the money supply continues to grow at 6 percent per annum. If our theory, which we use to relate unemployment, the money supply, and government expenditures, is incorrect, the odds in favor may not be as stated. Alternatively, if the money supply grows at 8 percent instead of 6 percent, then again the statement of the odds in favor are incorrect. The odds are now, say, 10:1.

Economists/econometricians cannot predict political (or other exogenous) behavior

Let us suppose a businessman or the government of the day asks for a prediction of, say, next year's gross national product (GNP). They do not want a conditional forecast; they want to know what GNP *will* be. The economist can provide a prediction, an *un*conditional forecast, but it is not very reliable, even if he restricts himself to a prediction of the chances of getting various levels of GNP. The reason is quite simply that, in order to make a prediction of GNP, the economist must "predict" the future values of other variables representing the circumstances in which a conditional forecast is made. Thus in the example about unemployment and the money supply, the economist must "predict" the future rate of growth in the money supply in order to be able to predict odds in favor of various unemployment rates. But here's the rub! We do not know how to predict such variables which are in the control of political (or other) forces "outside" the economic system. Economists and econometricians have no theory explaining such variables. All our theory can do is show us how to relate our variables of interest to business or government, like GNP or unemployment rates, to other such "exogenous" variables, like the money supply,[1] which, as it were, drive the economy from the outside, that is determine the values of GNP and so on, but are not themselves determined on the inside by the economy.

What is worse is that these exogenous variables are not random variables either. We cannot, except by guessing, specify the odds in favor of a change in the money supply or in government expenditure. If we could, that is, if government expenditure were a random variable, we would be able to give odds in favor of changes in GNP by using our theory to relate government expenditure to changes in GNP. If we *knew* with confidence what government policy is going to be, we could predict with equal confidence the odds in favor of given amounts of unemployment, and so on. But we cannot *know* what government policy will be. Nor can we have very much confidence in government predictions of their policy, since they quite naturally reserve the right to change their policies without notice.

One of the major advantages of micro- over macroeconomic forecasts is that the "exogenous variables" for micro problems, which are mainly laws of property rights and institutional details—such as the banking system, transportation facilities, available technology, and so on—are either constant for long periods or change very slowly and steadily. In contrast, macro policy variables—such as government expenditures and the

---

[1] These statements in the text about the *money supply* being "exogenous" are far too strong: What is exogenous or unpredictable, in the sense of observing no rational or explicable rules, is central bank behavior, for example, the policies of the Bank of England or the (U.S.) Federal Reserve: It is the behavior of politicians or their officials that is "exogenous."

money supply—change frequently and unpredictably.

Very simply, we conclude by saying that conditional forecasts are scientifically useful statements, whereas predictions are only as good as our guesses about the future values of such exogenous variables as government expenditure or the money supply. Since we have no way of evaluating the odds in favor of our guesses being correct, we have no way of setting odds in favor of our predictions. Economic predictions are guesses, although "educated" guesses.

Macro, misbegotten son of Micro—or the misuse of index numbers

So far, the loose definitions of micro- and macroeconomics have served us well. What, more precisely, is the connection (and lack of it) between micro and macro theory and the difference between them?

Strictly, or logically, we should be able to derive macro from micro theory. Micro theory is concerned with the "small-scale" behavior of individuals and firms within and between markets. Macro theory is concerned with "large-scale," "aggregate" variables like national income, investment, total consumption, and so on. If we have a theory about the way in which individuals behave, then, it might seem, macro relationships could be obtained by "adding up" the individual actions to get economy-wide totals, or "aggregates." Aggregate consumption (a macro variable), for example, is nothing more than the sum of everyone's consumption of all goods and services. Industrial investment is the aggregation or "adding up" of the investments by individual firms or other organizations. National income is the aggregation or "adding up" of everyone's income.

There is a weakness in this method. Although we can add expenditures in *money* terms, we cannot add physical/technical items of consumption or investment. We can add 20p worth of apples to 25p worth of oranges, but we cannot add apples and oranges. We can add thousands of pounds of investment expenditure on equipment of varying kinds, but we cannot add a machine tool to a printing press. Such difficulties are solved in economics by "index numbers," abstractions which enable us to *represent* a "quantity" of investment, of consumption, etc.

The basic idea is that if the index number, say, doubles, *all* the physical quantities of the individual items in the index double; for example, the number of printing presses of a given type, the number of machine tools, tons of bolts, tons of steel, and so on. Thus, all macro variables are index numbers.

This is not as dubious as it sounds, for economists are always dealing with index numbers, even in microeconomics. The market for wheat has to be discussed in terms of index numbers because there are different varieties and qualities of wheat, and each quality of each variety has its price. Consequently, in order to discuss the wheat market, an economist has to define a price index and a quantity index for wheat. If he were to forecast an increase in the "price" of "wheat" of, say, 10 percent, he is forecasting a 10 percent increase in the prices of each quality and type of wheat. However, if it is necessary for some purpose to distinguish between different types of wheat, the economist must disaggregate ("separate out") the wheat market into its components and define separate indices for each.

Macro "variables" differ in degree but not in type from micro "variables." Both are index numbers, but macro variables involve aggregations over *many more* different items than micro variables. Micro indices might represent individual "shirts," or cotton materials, or carbon steel, or even ferrous products; macro variables will aggregate all shirts, food, health care, shoes, holidays, and so on. It is the very wide spread of types of commodities in macro indices which make their use dangerous, not that they are indices. The danger lies in the (usually implied) assumption that the components of the index move proportionately. For if the components do move divergently, the index no longer represents the aggregation of the individual items. We may label this difficulty the "index number problem."

Let us suppose we have agreed on the choice of index numbers to represent our macro variables. We now come to an extremely difficult problem—indeed, as yet unsolved, except for some particular cases. Suppose we know the relationship between quantities demanded and the incomes of individual consumers in the "shirt," "potato," "health," "car," or other markets. The question quite simply is: How can we use this information to obtain the relationship between the *index* of aggregate consumption and the *index* of aggregate income? Most of what economists know about this problem is negative, that is, they know when you *cannot* derive a simple (or easily described) relationship between aggregates, even when the micro relationships are themselves very simple. In general, this difficulty can be characterized by saying that the two macro indices do not provide enough information. One aspect of this problem is that the observed *relationship* between, say, an *index* of consumption and an *index* of income will change ("shift," as economists say) with changes in the distribution of income, i.e., the variation of income over the population, even if the general level remains constant. For example, if with a given distribution of incomes, the relationship between the observed indices of consumption and income were such that each 10 percent increase in income raised consumption by 8 percent, a change in the distribution of income might alter the *relationship* between the indices so that each 10 percent increase in income raised consumption by only 6 percent. In such circumstances, if one wished to forecast changes in the index of consumption one would need to know not only the change in the *index* of income, but also the change in the distribution of income and how such changes would affect the consumption *index*.

Another important difference between micro and macro relationships is that whereas micro relationships are usefully treated as being independent of each other, macro relationships cannot. Consider a single consumer deciding how to spend his income. In microanalysis we may ignore the fact that his demand for goods provides, indirectly, a demand for his own labor services—to the extent that the farmer consumes his own food, the solicitor handles his own legal affairs, the businessman buys his firm's products. In macroanalysis, however, we cannot ignore the fact that total demand by all consumers directly affects the demand for their combined labor services. Each individual in an economy is a consumer and a provider of labor and savings. Individual decisions to work less, for example, directly affect individual decisions about spending and saving. In macro models the aggregate effects of these spending and saving decisions affect decisions about work, which in turn affect decisions on spending and saving.

Macro limitations—or, To aggregate or not to aggregate?

The power of macroeconomic analysis, its usefulness, lies in this dependence between aggregate relationships. Macroanalysis, by sacrificing the details of micro markets through aggregation, is able to focus on the interaction between consumption and work, saving and investment, money and output. Macroanalysis, therefore, is a powerful tool for handling some problems of special interest to politicians, but a dangerous one, as we have seen and shall see.

One of its chief dangers is to confuse a macro problem with micro problems, or at least to ignore the micro aspects of a macro problem. A truly macro problem is one in which the macro indices accurately represent the aggregates because the real components of the index move in the same way: For example, a proportionate underemployment of all resources, not only labor, but also capital and materials and energy, is a situation we might loosely describe as a general downturn in business activity. Another requirement of a truly macro problem is that the situation must be capable of being analyzed in terms of macro (aggregate) variables only, that is, we do not need to supplement our information on aggregate income, consumption, etc., with information on the individual variation of income and consumption over the population. With a 10 percent increase in aggregate income, it has been found that the consumption of some goods like food normally increases by less than 10 percent, whereas for other goods like cars consumption increases by more than 10 percent. Consequently, even with a 10 percent increase in everyone's income, the proportions of items in the consumption aggregate shift, so that the index is no longer representative of total consumption. For small changes in income, these differential effects can be ignored.

One way of handling a problem of this type is to "disaggregate" macro variables, that is, to decompose the total into subtotals. Total consumption can be divided into household goods and food, services, cars, durable goods like washing machines, and housing. By moving toward aggregations composed of fewer varieties of items, the "index number problem" can be mitigated. But this approach has a serious drawback because very quickly the number of relationships becomes so large that even the largest of modern computers cannot "solve" or "estimate" the system. The macroeconomist is often caught between the Scylla of the index number problem and the Charybdis of a system which cannot be "solved," or decomposed.

So far I have tried to show how micro and macro theory are logically related. Unfortunately, as hinted in the subheading, macro theory was not developed by trying to aggregate micro relationships. It grew in the beginning on its own and independently of the development of micro theory. Early twentieth-century economic sages might have quipped "micro is micro, and macro is macro, and never the twain shall meet." The term "macro theory" is relatively modern, indeed post–World War II. It grew out of the "Keynesian" discussions, which were in turn stimulated by the earlier ideas about money and its relationship to the general price level and aggregate output as well as by the work by Professor Simon Kuznets at the (U.S.) National Bureau of Economic Research, who developed the first measures of national income statistics, mainly during the 1920s and 1930s. This early work was primarily "institutional" in nature, that is, the emphasis was on collecting statistics and data on the economy as a whole and seeing if any empirical relationships could be found. The existing economic theory at the time had little to say about these newly measured "macro variables."

Perhaps it is surprising that serious efforts to establish the micro foundations of macro theory did not develop until after World War II.[2] I believe that it is because of these historical antecedents that there is a constant temptation for macro theorists to develop their ideas in a micro vacuum.[3] Indeed, some controversies in macroeconomic theory seem to lose sight

[2]A good example is an excellent text by Professor Don Patinkin, entitled *Money, Interest, and Prices, An Integration of Monetary and Value Theory,* 2nd ed. (New York: Harper and Row, 1965). Professor Patinkin mentions in the preface to the first edition that the text was an outgrowth of his doctoral dissertation at the University of Chicago in 1947. Part 1 is headed *Micro-Economics* and part 2, headed *Macro-Economics,* does not begin until page 199.

[3]Professor L. M. Lachmann presents an amusing discussion of this issue in *Macro-economic Thinking and the Market Economy* (London: Institute of Economic Affairs, Hobart Paper 56, 1973).

of even the central idea: the concentration on the interdependence between relationships by "aggregating out" the micro details. Thus, macroeconomists, by talking about "consumers," "investors," "workers," and so on, may forget that *every* individual is a consumer, a worker, an investor, and so on. Worse than that: macro relationships are sometimes hypothesized which are at variance with well-tested *micro* theory, such as early versions of the relationship between consumption, income, and interest rates. I suggest most macro theorists would agree that the failures of macroeconomic analysis stem almost entirely from neglecting its micro foundations, for example, the difficulties with aggregate investment and the lack of attention paid to the supply side of macro models. However, while there is general agreement in principle that more micro theory should be incorporated into the formulation of macro models, there are many technical difficulties which need to be overcome before a successful incorporation can be achieved. One of these difficulties is the index-number problem discussed above.

Policy making requires forecasting—based on measurement, not surmise

Rational policy decisions require forecasting. For if we are to choose between several courses of action, we must forecast their outcomes. If a firm is contemplating whether to invest or not and if so in what equipment and by how much, it will need to know the outcomes if it is to be able to make an informed choice between the alternatives. If a government is contemplating the imposition of a wealth tax, an economically informed decision will require a forecast of the probable effects. Even taking no action and accepting the *status quo* is a policy decision, so that the decision to do nothing in the face of requests for "positive action" requires macro information (as well as micro, of course) for making a rational economic decision. The knowledge on which informed decisions are made is obtained from economic forecasts.

The firm or the government asks the question: If the circumstances are such and such, and if I take action A, or B, or C, what are the odds in favor of the various possible outcomes? Let us examine two examples.

(i) Cereals

By the third quarter of 1972 world agricultural experts realized that the prices of cereals had risen substantially. Was this a temporary occurrence, or had there been a permanent shift in demand and supply relationships (equations)? Had supply fallen? or had demand increased? In either case, what was the explanation? The answers would indicate the appropriate policy action by both exporting and importing countries. Careful analysis of the data indicated clearly that the decrease in the supply of wheat which caused the price rise was due to government policies of the United States, Canada, Australia, and even the USSR. Between them, these four countries account for 85 percent of world trade in wheat. Governmental (not private) decisions substantially reduced the acreage of land in wheat after 1968. In 1970 Canadian acreage was half the 1969 level and the U.S. acreage in 1970 was back to the 1948–52 levels, that is, about 60 million acres withdrawn from production. According to official statements, the "cutbacks were ordered or induced by national authorities in order to cope with production in excess of available outlets."[4]

(ii) Oil

Consider another example. During the latter half of 1973 and the Arab oil embargo, many U.S. politicians were claiming (or rather asserting without evidence) that allowing the petrol market to respond to the situation would not solve the problem. It would not increase output, there would be no decrease in demand, the price of petrol would rise from 40¢ per gallon to $1.00 or $2.00, and the burden on "the poor" would be intolerable since they would have to spend an additional $100 per month to run their cars. In response to these supposed "facts," many politicians recommended rationing, a petrol price freeze, and nationalization of the industry. The Nixon administration created the Federal Energy Office (FEO) to handle the "crisis." The crisis, if there ever was one, is now past, but the FEO is firmly established for the indefinite future.

During the apparent crisis, the FEO managed to make a dif-

---

[4]E. Reubens, "The Food Shortage is not Inevitable," *Challenge* ("The Magazine of Economic Affairs"—White Plains, New York), March-April 1974, p. 51.

ficult situation much worse by restricting the supply and impeding the efficient distribution of crude oil, raising the average cost of refining, ordering the wrong proportions of crude oil distillates to be produced, sending too much petrol to some states and not enough to others, and precipitating (in conjunction with another federal agency) a nationwide lorry drivers' (truckers') strike in which one person was killed and many injured.

In contrast to this response of government to politicians' theories, let us examine the situation from the economist's viewpoint. First, on the facts, it is clearly not true that an increase in price has no effect on the output of petrol. Despite the lack of refinery capacity at the time of the crisis (caused by earlier governmental policies), supply did increase and could have increased even more without interference. Econometric estimates indicated that for every 1 percent increase in the price of crude oil the supply would also increase by 1 percent within a year. An econometric analysis of demand[5] I conducted with two colleagues essentially agreed with other econometric studies in concluding that for every 10 percent increase in the price of petrol, the quantity demanded would fall by 7 percent; the price of 55¢ per gallon (the current price in mid-1974) would equate supply and demand, with neither shortage nor surplus; and the maximum burden on the poor (even using a very generous definition of the term) would be $20.00 per year (not $100 per month). It is now clear that the econometric analysis was on target and that if the oil market had been allowed to adjust itself in the usual way there would have been no "crisis." (Indeed, few people would even have known there was supposed to be a "crisis.") A final irony is that government policies increased U.S. reliance on Arab oil from 4 percent of total demand in 1970 to over 16 percent in 1975: So much for "Project Independence."

The two alternatives to econometrics

Let us now turn our attention to examples of macro policy and forecasting. By now the reader will have gathered that, far

[5]Professors James Ramsey, Robert Rasche, and Bruce Allen, "An Initial Analysis of the Private and Commercial Demand for Gasoline," *Review of Economics and Statistics,* November 1975.

from econometrics being connected solely with macroanalysis, macro problems provide only a part of the subject matter of econometrics. In addition, he will have acquired a more sophisticated idea of the role of econometrics in the study of macroeconomics. This role is clarified by comparing the economist's scientific approach through econometrics to the existing alternatives of what I shall call naïve prediction and ad hoccery or ad hoc construction.

There is a striking irony in the respective approaches of the econometrician and the politician in examining macro policy issues. It is aptly illustrated by Professor I. M. D. Little who had in mind economics as it is (or was, but possibly still is) mishandled by British economists who advise ministers:

> Economic theory teaches one how economic magnitudes are related, and how very complex and involved these relationships are. Non-economists tend to be too academic. They abstract too much from the real world. No-one can think about economic issues without some theory, for the facts and relationships are too involved to organise themselves: they do not simply fall into place.
>
> But if the theorist is untutored, he is apt to construct a very partial theory which blinds him to some of the possibilities. Or he falls back on some old and over-simple theory, picked up from somewhere or other. He is also, I believe, apt to interpret the past naïvely. *Post hoc, ergo propter hoc* is seldom an adequate economic explanation. I was sometimes shocked by the naïve sureness with which very questionable bits of economic analysis were advanced in Whitehall.[6]

The contrast between recommended econometric procedures and current practice is illustrated by a discussion of the two most common alternatives to econometrics, naïve prediction and ad hoc model construction. Both approaches have been used at various times by business and governments in the United States, the United Kingdom, and elsewhere.

(a) Naïve prediction

Naïve prediction applies a simple methodology. Either the predictor estimates some relationship and *assumes* that the

---

[6]Professor I. M. D. Little, "The Economist in Whitehall," *Lloyds Bank Review*, April 1957. *"Post hoc ergo propter hoc"* is literally "After this,

same results will hold in the future; or he predicts values by using currently observed trends in economic variables over time, for example, he says next year's income will be equal to this year's plus 5 percent. There is no attempt to provide a theoretical model in order to understand the observed relationships. There is no concern for identification and little for separating out the individual effects of exogenous variables. The procedure produces only "predictions," not conditional forecasts, since the idea of "conditioning circumstances" is ignored. We have already seen that "prediction" as opposed to "forecasts" is no more than a form of guessing.

This approach is relatively costless and can be quite useful, but only under very restrictive assumptions. First, we must be confident that the underlying system generating the observed relationships *will* continue in the future. In other words, we assume that the micro components within the macro aggregates do not change in such a way as to alter the relationships between the macro variables. If the macroeconomic system changes, we do not know which changes in the economic environment are important and which are not. And, even if we do know, we still do not know how the relationships will be affected. Because no theory is brought to bear on the problems, we have no way of responding to changes in the system. The naïve prediction approach is like fitting a smooth curve to a sequence of points on a graph and extending it beyond the last observed point with no reason (theory) to suppose the trend continues unchanged but only *assuming* it does.

A further obvious objection to this procedure is that, having obtained a "good fit" over a given historical set of data, we are not justified in extending the predictions beyond the historical experience, even if we know that the underlying system is unchanged. This is because the results of naïve prediction are not valid outside the observed range. If, for example, total consumption is observed to increase by four-fifths of the increase in income for income per capita in the range of £1,000 to £4,000 over a period, we cannot *on this information alone* assert that if income per capita increases from £4,000 to £5,000

therefore because of this." It refers to the logical fallacy of assuming that A must have caused B if A preceded B.

consumption will increase by £800. For without a theory which asserts that consumption increases with increases in income, we have no way of knowing from the observed data alone that increases in income beyond £4,000 might decrease consumption. And, even if we have such a theory, we still could not predict an increase of £800, since we would still have no theory which indicated that the rate of increase in consumption to increases in income is the same above £4,000 as below.

Another objection is that naïve prediction uses simple relationships between highly aggregated variables. We have already seen (section 4, p. 30) the difficulties in trying to summarize in this way a complex set of relationships between a large number of micro variables. In naïve prediction, the indices are too broad and do not incorporate enough of the underlying micro information. The only way in which to handle complicated systems involving a large number of variables is to use theory in order to go "behind," as it were, the appearances, so that we may express the relationship between, for example, interest rates and investment in terms of the interactions between micro markets.

Thus, the relationship between interest rates and amount of investment depends upon a complex network of interrelationships which can be summarized in terms of the direct interaction between three sets of equations. The first involves interactions between rates of interest and investment goods, which depend upon the demand for and supply of the existing stock of capital goods. These equations interact with the second set of equations, the demand for and supply of investment capital, which is affected in turn by the demand for and supply of money. These interactions are the most direct; I have excluded indirect interactions which relate consumption, income levels, and government expenditure to the interaction between investment and interest rates. To understand an observed relationship between investment and interest rates we must therefore consider the interactions throughout most of the economy.

Although it is a relatively simple process (for the statistician) to estimate or fit a relationship to a given set of data, the main question for the forecaster is the confidence he can accumulate in using such a relationship and the extent to which it provides useful forecasts to problems and circumstances not previously observed. Macroeconomics is concerned almost entirely with *changes* in an economy and extensions *beyond* experience, so that naïve prediction models are simply not relevant. Consider, for example, the imposition of a value-added tax or a wealth tax, increasing the money supply more than ever before, record levels of government expenditures, and the development of new technology: All these are *new* developments on which experience (i.e., *old* knowledge) can shed no dependable light.

The defenders of naïve prediction will claim that in practice the procedure produces fairly good predictions. Let us agree for now that for short periods (say, one year), and for some variables (like income and consumption), naïve prediction procedures may give "reasonable" predictions. But this result is fortuitous. It is due to the inherent short-run stability of some variables, such as consumption, and, since the last war, to the dominance of "growth" over short-run variations about a steady-growth path. In a period of sustained steady growth, prediction is easy. But it is then also hardly enlightening. If this year's consumption is last year's plus 5 percent, it is not difficult to predict next year's. But, and this is the rub, what evidence is there, what analysis or theory indicates that next year *will* be like last year?

The degree of success and failure of naïve prediction procedures may be attributed directly to the extent to which steady growth is the main determinant of a variable. These procedures, therefore, break down at the very time they are most needed: when the economy moves off a steady-growth path, when governments make significant policy changes, or there are substantial shifts in overseas markets. The most crucial test of any forecasting procedure is whether it correctly forecasts "turning points," that is, *changes* in direction of economic variables. Deficiencies in naïve prediction tend to be obscured by the large number of "agreements" between model and data, especially when almost any model would have made reasonable predictions, namely when the economy is growing steadily. These comments emphasize the importance of the scientific method which focuses on trying to reject a theory, to discover forecasting errors, not simply to record the number of agreements between data and prediction.

The significance of this discussion is that naïve prediction is still used in industry and government in Britain. For example, "trend projection" is a simple form of naïve prediction indulged in by practically everyone (including the author in his weaker moments). The idea is that predictions of future coal or oil consumption, or electricity demand, or population growth, or increases in pollution, or portion of GDP controlled by government, and so on ad infinitum, can all be "predicted" by projecting into the future the rate of growth during some recent period. Trend projections are easily made and easily understood: Anyone with paper and pencil can make one; so nearly everyone does. But what is produced at so little cost in intellectual effort and understanding of the world is worth precisely that: practically nothing.

However, trend projections do have their uses, and that is why they are so popular: They provide a rationale, an excuse if you prefer, for action. Trend projections are usually prefaced by: "If we do not do something, then by the year ——— (reader's choice[7]) disaster will occur." The public is constantly bombarded by such claims made by government agencies, bureaucrats, firms, unions, and special-interest groups of all kinds.

(b) Ad hoccery

The next procedure might be termed ad hoc construction (ahc). Ahc procedures have been used by the National Institute of Economic and Social Research and especially by the Treasury. They combine the methodology of naïve prediction with the use of "intuitive insights" and nonquantified (often nonquantifiable) information. Usually what happens is that the predictor does not believe his statistical estimates, so he arbitrarily changes them to bring them more in accord with his current prejudices. Built into such a model are the forecaster's current sentiments and preconceptions, based on haphazard information about what people may or may not do or have done. Such procedures are based on the idea that the "predictor knows," although he does *not* know the basis for his

[7]The year 2001 is currently very popular, since the years 1980, 1984, are now far too close for the comfort of the trend predictor, because the refutation of the prediction is almost certain and the prediction might be remembered. 2001 is sufficiently far away so that the trend prediction can provide a "dramatic disaster" and the risk of being proven wrong in the predictor's lifetime is slight.

"knowledge"; nor does he test his intuition. Indeed, the situation is worse than this since such models are constructed by teams, not by individuals. Different people get precedence from time to time in pursuing their intuition depending on their "successes" in the previous period. For example, imagine that Mr. Sooth and Mr. Sayer are two members of a team making macroeconomic predictions and that for some time Mr. Sooth's "hunches," or "feelings," about the way the economy might proceed in the next few months have been closer to what happened that those of Mr. Sayer. With this experience, whenever our two gentlemen predictors disagree over their "hunches," Mr. Sooth will most likely have the last word. But, if Mr. Sayer runs into a winning streak, then his "hunches" will get priority. Unfortunately, by that time Mr. Sooth may be back on a winning streak. A close analogy is to imagine a pair of roulette gamblers who agree that whichever of them won the last round decides the bet for the next.

The public may be forgiven for thinking that this approach is the best way to make forecasts. In our daily experience intuition does not usually lead us too far astray in ordering our own affairs. But the discussion in this paper should raise serious doubts about the efficacy of this comforting idea. First, learning from our mistakes, especially by governments, can be very costly. Secondly, the economy is so complex that such naïve learning procedures are useless. Thirdly, since we are more concerned with *changes* in the system and extending our predictions *beyond* the region of our experience, these intuitive procedures provide little scope for handling the interesting problems. More important, ad hoccery cannot be evaluated by its success in predicting. There is no way of telling whether the model provides good predictions, or someone's intuition was *fortuitously* correct. With ad hoccery we cannot estimate the odds in favor or against our predictions because of the arbitrary changes in the estimates of the coefficients. Consequently, we are no longer able to evaluate the accuracy of our predictions and how they will change from sample period to sample period. All we can do is to record the historical degree of success of the predictor in the *past*. Since there is no theory, there is no reason why this historical success will indicate success in the *future*. We might be able to claim that, over a given period one group of Treasury men had better success than another; but that is all we can say, and no valid inference can be drawn from this experience. Further, if the observer has enough patience to wait, he will discover that the group with the best historical success usually changes (unpredictably!) from period to period.

These comments explain why both the detractors and defenders of any given macro policy, such as an incomes policy, can usually find some evidence to support their positions. Frequently, both sides can find data both for and against the efficacy of any policy. In these cases each party "explains" the contrary data by referring to "special circumstances." Arguments along these lines cannot be resolved logically and can be continued ad infinitum.

The real thing—from number fudging to fact facing

In clear contrast to naïve prediction and ad hoccery are the "econometric procedures" discussed in section 3. The key differences are, first, that econometric procedures recognize the distinction between *conditional* forecasts and predictions, second, they are designed to forecast not outcomes themselves but the *odds* in favor or against the occurrence of the outcomes, because they recognize the stochastic nature of economic theory, and, third, they incorporate in the forecasting procedure as much economic *theory* as possible. By these means the econometrician can respond to accumulated evidence and thereby modify the theoretical structure efficiently and scientifically. The forecaster himself and, much more important, other researchers can monitor and evaluate the learning process, thereby enabling the forecaster to build a better "model" over time. The better model is that derived from the better theory. The better theory is the one which provides on average closer predictions of more variables and indicates in more detail the complex relationships between the variables; in short, *the better theory provides a better understanding of the world.*

Before proceeding with a discussion of the status of existing macro models, two issues must be raised. First, the comparison drawn above between naïve prediction/ad hoc models and econometric models is one between "best practices," as it were. Thus, to the extent that an "econometric" model does not use the best statistical procedures, to the extent that it must rely on noneconometric predictions for the conditioning (exogenous) variables, and to the extent that economic theory is not used, econometric models will be subject to the *same* criticisms as naïve prediction models and ad hoc models.

Second, the usual situation is one in which a model will contain elements of all three approaches. Some relationships in a model might be predicted by naïve prediction methods, others by ad hoc procedures, and some relationships forecast by econometric methods. But even in those relationships originally estimated by econometric methods, there is, as we shall see, strong pressure on the forecaster/predictor to "adjust" his estimates by ad hoc methods.

The most purely econometric models are those constructed by researchers primarily interested in developing and testing economic theory per se, not in providing predictions of GNP, price levels, etc., for general consumption. Such research models are usually small: They have only a relatively small number of relationships and tend to concentrate on one particular aspect of the whole economy, for example, the money market, determinants of aggregate consumption, and so on. Some macro relationships are reasonably well understood, for example, consumption; others, like inventory levels and labor supply, are only partially and tentatively understood. Clearly, research-orientated models do not begin to provide the scope of detailed predictions usually demanded by the governmental and private consumers of macro-model output.

Consequently, in the face of a demand for detailed and numerous macro predictions, and in the light of the incomplete and very uneven development of macro theory, it is natural to expect that naïve prediction and ad hoc construction will be used to fill the macro-theory vacuum. Further, given the strong interdependencies between various relationships in the economy, the "practical macro-modeller," that is, the one trying to satisfy the demand for macro predictions, often finds that he can make "reasonable" short-run predictions more quickly by exercising his judgment and changing estimates in an ad hoc fashion; but the cost is to lose all the potential advantages of the econometric approach, the most important of which is to learn from one's mistakes.

The "practical macro-modeller" faces a dilemma. Imagine that Mr. M. M. has just produced a pure econometric macro model, the month is April, and the inventory relationship is obviously wrong, that is, the hypothetical inventory relationship has been tested and overwhelmingly rejected by the data. The pure researcher need only sigh and return to the drawing board in hope of eventually discovering a better relationship for inventories. But the practical macro-modeller, Mr. M. M., knows that by the end of May he has to produce "reasonable" estimates of a wide variety of national income variables, for if he does not his competitors will; he knows that his current inventory estimates are causing problems elsewhere in the model, and that the odds against a large shift in direction of the overall economy are reasonably low. What to do? A typical response would be to replace the failed econometric relationship by a naïve predictive one (at least it fits the known data!), ignore the fact that some other relationships, while not in accord with economic theory, seem to fit the data "reasonably well," especially after a few judicious alterations of some of the coefficients, and then use the "adjusted" model to predict. If Mr. M. M. is very skillful and his bet on the odds against a major shift pays off, he will produce figures for the next half-year which are "reasonable," i.e., most people knowledgeable in national income statistics would not be unduly surprised by Mr. M. M.'s predictions. Mr. M. M. has survived to fight another day.

The record of the model builders

With these issues in mind, let us consider briefly the record of a few of the practical model builders. The intention is not to provide an extensive review of even the most familiar models, but merely to illustrate the various arguments developed in this paper.

A paper by Professor D. J. Smyth and J. C. K. Ash[8] was severely critical of Treasury and NIESR macro models during the 1950s and 1960s:

> It is disconcerting that the forecasts [of the Treasury and NIESR] show no tendency to improve over time; this is in

[8]"The Accuracy of the United Kingdom Annual Macro-Economic Forecasts" (Discussion Paper no. 30, Department of Economics, University of Reading,

contrast to the behaviour of comparable forecasts in the Netherlands where predictive accuracy has improved over the period 1953–63. There, such improvements may be attributed largely to two factors. First, improvements in the basic model underlying the forecasts: in particular the substitution of an essentially dynamic model for a static one. Secondly, increasing use of econometric techniques.

And they rub in their criticism:

It is interesting that the two series for which the National Institute's forecasts appear to be superior to the Treasury's are stocks and imports, for it is for these two series that the National Institute used a certain amount of sophistication in the application of econometric techniques during the period of our study.

As the reader will probably have guessed from these quotations, the Treasury and NIESR models are a mixture of naïve prediction, ad hoc construction, and econometric models, although the role of econometrics is a minor and recent innovation. Nevertheless, it is clear from the discussion above that the pressures on both groups to produce a variety of national income estimates at frequent intervals will militate strongly against a substantial increase in the relevance of the econometric approach.

Professor Lawrence Klein,[9] basing his analysis on the much more accurate and detailed U.S. and Canadian data, claims that good econometric forecasts should reach accuracy of a chance of one in ten for forecast errors within plus or minus 1 percent for levels of variables, plus or minus 10 percent for changes in variables, plus or minus one index point for price indices, and plus or minus one-half of an index point for the unemployment rate. For example, Dr. Michael Evans,[10] in evaluating forecasts made with the Wharton EFU model,[11] notes that the average error in GNP quarterly forecasts (be-

1971), p. 18; reprinted in *Forecasting the UK Economy* (Saxon House/Lexington Books, 1973).

[9]"The Precision of Econometric Prediction: Standards, Achievement, Potential" (Paper presented at the Outlook Conference, United States, 1972).

[10]*Macro Economic Activity, Theory, Forecasting and Control* (New York: Harper and Row, 1969). P. 429.

[11]The Wharton EFU model is a macro model of the U.S. economy produced by the Wharton School of Business, University of Pennsylvania.

tween 1963 and 1965) was approximately ½ percent, and states that in a simulation experiment[12] with the model over a 48-quarter period the model correctly tracked the U.S. downturns in 1954, 1958, and 1960, and even reflected the minor decline in 1956. It further tracked current economic conditions in that it did not turn down anywhere else. The quarter-to-quarter correspondence was not precise in many cases; a major example was the failure of the model to follow the full extent of the 1955–57 capital goods boom. However, it did reflect all turning points correctly and did not "predict" any which did not occur.

Only a short time has elapsed between the development of the first U.S. macro models in the early 1950s and attainments in the 1970s.[13] In the beginning, even U.S. forecasts were little better than naïve forecasting methods in short-run prediction, but the scientific method of the econometric approach has enabled the forecasters to build better models by rejecting the inferior. In the United States and Canada, the Brookings models, the MIT-FRB models, and the RDX[14] models of the Bank of Canada are examples of successful econometric macro-model building. The production of larger and increasingly complicated macro models is now at the stage in which experiments are being conducted in developing a world econometric model through Project Link, a brainchild of Professor Lawrence Klein.

[12]A simulation experiment of a macro model provides a useful check on its predictive capabilities. The procedure is to generate *all* the values of the endogenous variables (i.e., the model-determined variables) from the known values of the exogenous variables (conditioning variables) and the estimated coefficients. If the generated values of the endogenous variables are "close" to the observed values, the model can be regarded as a useful tool for forecasting provided the assumptions under which the coefficients were estimated continue to hold. For example, a significant change in the operation of financial institutions would render the model useless.

[13]In Britain the history of macro models is even more recent. For example, the London Business School model, in operation for less than fifteen years, began a detailed description of the financing of the public sector and included the money supply as an endogenous variable *only in* 1972. The Treasury model was not even computerized until 1970!

[14]The MIT-FRB macro model is jointly sponsored by the Massachusetts Institute of Technology and the Federal Reserve Board in Boston. The RDX macro model is sponsored by the Bank of Canada although much of the research on the model is due to economists at the Universities of Toronto and British Columbia.

The idea is to see if the forecasting performance of each country's own models can be improved by "linking" them together through a model of international trade relations. But the world model will be only as good as its constituent parts, and many of them are not very useful because of all the arguments raised above, together with the relative scarcity of macro data, not to mention macro-modeling experience and expertise in most of the countries involved.

This record of progress, however, has been possible only by paying increasing attention to the micro aspects of macro models. To derive a stable macro system we must understand the underlying micro relationships. The "Phillips curve," for example, was thought to be a well-known observed (not theoretical) relationship between the rate of unemployment and the rate of change in money wages. It is also well known that this empirical relationship is different in various countries and has been shifting over time. Unfortunately, notwithstanding the constant change in the Phillips curve, most politicians act as if it were fixed and stable.[15]

To understand why the Phillips curve is shifting we must relate the aggregate unemployment to the degree of excess supply over demand in each individual micro market making up the aggregate. A simple shift in the relative sizes of various industries, for example, would shift an observed Phillips curve, because the relative weight given to industries in which employment shifts dramatically with changes in the level of economic activity would alter (for example, a decline in construction relative to the computer industry). The reader will now recognize this difficulty as an illustration of the index number problem discussed earlier in this section.

Macroanalysis can provide useful summary information about the behavior of entire economies only if it is supplemented by detailed microanalysis which enables us to anticipate poten-

---

[15]Milton Friedman, *Unemployment versus Inflation?: An Evaluation of the Phillips Curve* (London: Institute of Economic Affairs, Occasional Paper 44, 1975); *Inflation and Unemployment* (London: IEA, Occasional Paper 51, 1977). The Phillips curve has not been a useful concept for over a decade despite numerous attempts by scholars on both sides of the Atlantic to rescue it, e.g., Professors E. S. Phelps (United States) and M. Parkin (United Kingdom), to name but two.

tial *shifts* in the macro relationships and to anticipate situations in which the macro indices no longer "represent" the corresponding aggregates of micro variables, such as investment, the price level, and, especially important, unemployment.

Econometric macro models, as I have tried to illustrate, improve their predictive performance over time—even if they begin at a naïve prediction level of sophistication. But naïve and ad hoc prediction do not improve their performance over time; nor can they. There is nothing magical about this but much hard work. The first essential difference between econometric and other approaches is that the former is thoroughly embedded in economic theory and can be modified with advances in theoretical understanding.

Although econometric models can be used by firms, unions, and government for forecasting and policy analysis, their primary role is as a vehicle for testing and advancing macroeconomic theory. Econometric models are much more concerned with trying to understand the structure and interrelationships of macro systems, whereas other predicting approaches are merely devices to "guess the future." However, except in broad outline and where rates of change in variables are modest, it is unfortunately true that economists still do not understand how the macroeconomy functions. I have been arguing, and trust that by now the reader has been persuaded, that no one else knows any more, and most a great deal less. Current government macroeconomic policy, therefore, can best be described as "Russian roulette."

Macro models try to incorporate the process of change

We have already seen that naïve predictions are valid only in a stable and unchanging environment and that the macro system is undergoing continuous change. Consequently, naïve prediction procedures can only be expected to provide reasonable forecasts for short periods of time (say, one year) without extensive modification. In practice, models used by naïve predictors undergo *continuous* (not just constant) modification; it is almost literally true that such models are altered day by day in a continuous effort to adapt them to an ever-changing world.

Econometric models, however, attempt to determine the

underlying structure. Macroeconomists try to analyze the effects of a *changing* environment. The more we uncover the micro components of the relationships between broad aggregates, the better we can discover stable relationships. The pursuit of this objective has led macroeconomists more and more toward the disaggregation of macro models and the incorporation of dynamic elements and the analysis of economies in disequilibrium. In short, economists are now trying to build macro models which incorporate the process of change, of adjustment to new circumstances. It is no longer thought adequate to be able to forecast the final effect of an increase in the money supply, i.e., the equilibrium result; it would clearly be helpful to forecast how the economy adjusts itself to the change, how it reacts and for how long. One aspect of the current debate between monetarists and the Keynesians, for example, is about the relative lengths of the time lags between implementing a fiscal or monetary policy and observing the effect. However, the extension of macro analysis beyond equilibria can be of more fundamental importance. Thus, the equilibrium result of a *once-for-all* increase in the money supply is to *lower* interest rates, whereas a *continuous increase* in the money supply which produces inflation *raises* interest rates. I am constantly amazed at the tenacity of public officials who insist that the money supply should be increased to lower interest rates when inflation is already at a high level.

The major contrast, in procedures and techniques, with naïve prediction is the full recognition in econometric methods of the complexity of interrelationships in economies and of the importance of "identification." Indeed, it is this complex interdependence of macro variables which characterizes the macroeconomic problem and establishes the inherent advantage of the econometric over other approaches.

The last few years, and more particularly 1975–76, have produced a set of real-world events which are proving stringent tests of all types of forecast. Simultaneous increasing unemployment and increasing rates of inflation are not explained by current conventional macro wisdom. A number of economists, such as Professors Harold Shapiro, Gottfried Haberler, Karl Brunner, David Laidler, and Ray Fair, have interesting and plausible ideas about the problem and there is evidence in support of some of their ideas; but there is as yet no generally accepted macro theory explaining the recent past. As I have emphasized, the test of a forecast comes when the economy unexpectedly does *not* continue to "go on as before."

Econometrics helps learning from experience

The reactions of econometric, naïve, and ad hoc construction forecasts and predictions to these new data illustrate many of my arguments about methodology. The naïve predictor's main tool is the "lead" indicator, a national income statistic which historically has been observed to change direction well in advance of the rest of the economy—for example, hours worked, unemployment claims, stock market prices, and corporate profits. Since December 1973 the main leading indicators have not only failed to indicate the rough magnitude of changes; they have been in the wrong direction. The reason is that the relationships underlying the lead indicators' past successes have changed. We have here another example of the identification problem.

Recall the wheat example in section 3. Suppose someone had discovered by simple observation of the past that the price of wheat each year was predicted by the date migratory birds went south; the later the date, the lower the price of wheat. What our imaginative observer might have been observing was that a dry autumn gave rise to warmer days thereby both increasing the wheat harvest and delaying bird migration. It is conceivable that the predictions might be accurate for a long period. But, as we have already noted, what if climatic changes were to lead to colder weather being associated with a dry autumn? or an improved fertilizer was introduced in wheat production? or technological improvements in industry raised consumer incomes? or the price of potatoes fell? or shipping costs for U.S. wheat rose? or...? In any of these cases, the old lead indicator would no longer be of use. And so it is with the lead indicators in the macroeconomy except that the possibilities for a change in underlying relationships are much larger.

Lead indicators are failing the predictive test. What can be done? How can someone who uses a lead indicator to forecast learn from his experience? All he can do is try to find a new indicator. But even if he does by examining past behavior, what confidence can he have in his procedure? How soon will it also prove unreliable?

The ad hoc construction predictors are in an even more difficult situation; all they can do is to replace one man's intuition by another's.

In contrast, econometric methods enable the economist to learn from the experience by discovering exactly where in the model the failure occurred and then, aided by theory, trying to discover the missing relationships in the rejected model. For example, macroeconomists know that the change in price of petrol has shifted U.S. demand for automobiles toward smaller cars. They will want to discover how such changes affect macro relationships between consumption and income. One of the chief current deficiencies in macroeconomic models is the inadequate attention paid to the supply side of markets. Professor Aaron Gordon of the University of California has said:

> The forecasters fell flat on their faces in predicting price changes because they didn't have any way of estimating sectoral supply scarcity.[16]

Economists in the United States are now working hard to rectify this gap in macro theory.

As a final example of the economist's reaction to recent events, let me cite Professor Kenneth Arrow, a Nobel prize winner in economics:

> The weakness in inflation theory goes right down to the micro-level, to the theory of price determination at the level of the individual firm.[17]

And what lies ahead for the economist trying to improve macro forecasts is indicated by Professor James Tobin:

> I'm afraid that we're in for a long period of slugging it out with a lot of complex problems.

Let me summarize the gist of my argument with a pungent

---

[16]I.e., because many supply relationships had been relatively fixed when the models were estimated, their effects on the other macro relationships had been ignored. "Theory Deserts the Forecasters," *Business Week,* June 29, 1974, p. 50. (Professor Gordon was president of the American Economic Association in 1975.)

[17]Ibid., p. 59.

quotation from Professor Paul Samuelson:[18]

> When I say that as an economist I am not very good at making economic forecasts, that sounds like modesty. But actually, it represents the height of arrogance. For I know that, bad as we are, we are better than anything else in heaven and earth at forecasting aggregate business trends—better than gypsy tea-leaf readers, Wall Street soothsayers and chartist technicians, hunch-playing heads of mail-order chains, or all-powerful heads of state.
>
> This is a statement based on empirical experience. Over the years, I have tried to keep track of various methods of forecasting, writing down in my little black book what people seem to be saying before the event, and then comparing their prediction with what happened. The result has been a vindication of the hypothesis that there is no efficacious substitute for economic analysis in business forecasting. Some maverick may hit a home run on occasion; but over the long season batting averages tend to settle down to a sorry level when the esoteric methods of soothsaying are relied upon.

---

[18]"Economic Forecasting and Science," *Michigan Quarterly Review,* October 1965, p. 277.

5. A Better Way to Understand the Economic World and Its Effects on You

In section 4, I compared micro and macro theory and indicated the connection between them. We have also now discovered that macro theory and macro forecasting (as distinct from prediction) can be of considerable use in governmental policy decisions, but that even the best state of the art of forecasting is far from perfect and that macroanalysis in untrained hands can be a dangerous tool.

From fumbling (macro) steps to best (micro) feet forward

Fortunately, many of the matters of prime importance for policy rest upon microanalysis and it is in this sphere that the economist can put his best foot forward. By comparison, macroanalysis has taken only a few stumbling steps. In any event, macro policy must work through micro relationships, through the decisions of individuals and firms, and it is usually those micro aspects which determine the effectiveness of macro policy.

The overall effectiveness of monetary policy, for example, depends upon the institutional context within which the policy is implemented and which determines how, and how quickly, an increase in money reaches individual decision-makers. Economists recognize that it is not enough to consider the simple aggregate effects; they must also consider the interactions between the domestic money supply and the international money market, the relative rates of disbursement of an increase in money to manufacturing investment, inventory stocks, building and plant investment, domestically-produced and imported consumer goods. Such analysis often reveals the harmful effects of what are misleadingly called "market imperfections": Interest-rate restrictions on mortgage lending institutions, hire-purchase restrictions, government-backed barriers to entry, and so on, distort and even nullify the anticipated benefits of an increase in the money supply. The gains to society from a return of emphasis in policy to the micro aspects of macro problems are considerable and far outweigh the potential benefits from a successful implementation of stabilization policy in trying to maintain steady full-employment growth without inflation.

Macro policies at best correct opposite errors;
little scope for initiating growth

It may seem that macro stabilization of the economy cannot be more ambitious than a reaction to minor short-run changes caused, for example, by changes in international trade conditions. All that macro stabilization policies can provide is counterbalancing expenditures and changes in the money supply to forecast changes in economic conditions. Stabilization is accomplished by varying a small number of instruments, such as the money supply, fiscal expenditures, etc., so that, at best, macro policies are merely *corrective* and have little scope for *initiating* growth.

However, even this modest recommendation is dangerous. In practice, there is evidence that it is governmental policies themselves, *including attempts at stabilization,* which are the prime sources of economic *instability*. And I do not exclude the 1930s depression from this charge. Professor Friedman, for example, has long held this view about monetary policy. Recently, Professor Otto Eckstein, who helped to pioneer the ideas of "fine-tuning" in the United States, concluded, on reviewing the evidence of the 1960s, that fine-tuning had been destabilizing, had increased inflation, but had had no discernible effect on real growth and unemployment.[1]

Driving a train by the rear window

Macro stabilization policies can be likened to driving a train by looking through the rear window (or steering a boat by its wake!). To continue the analogy, macro monetary and fiscal policies are the accelerator and brake of the engine; micro theory provides the linkups between the controls and the engine

[1]Quoted by Lindley Clark, "Can Taxes Fine Tune the Economy," *Imprimis* (Hillsdale College, Hillsdale, Michigan), March 1976.

and the wheels. More importantly, micro theory, especially the theory of property rights, provides the design of the engine in the first place. In short, macro policy uses the micro-provided controls to maintain an even speed in the face of variations in the gradient of the track.

In contrast, the intent, if not the effect, of centralized planning is to *control* the growth in the economy, not merely react to changes in the economy itself. The idea of "central planning" and control is based on the notion that, with a relatively small number of policy instruments, the government can set and realize desired rates of growth, low unemployment, and no inflation. Governments may indulge in this self-delusion indefinitely, but economic analysis shows clearly that basic economic forces still determine the path of the economy so that central control is seen to be an elaborate charade. If the basic economic and technological constraints to growth are recognized, central planning becomes an expensive and highly inefficient substitute for the market in allocating resources and stimulating growth. Few people realize the order of magnitude of effort required in trying to replace the market with planning. The commitment to the supposed benefits of planning stems mainly from ignorance of what it is that markets do and the efficiency with which they allocate resources. The more economic life changes and the faster the rate of technological change, the more efficient market methods relative to attempts at planning.

The price and wage control dilemmas during the Roman Empire provide an instructive example of the central planner's dilemma.[2] Inflation from the time of Augustus Caesar was created by an effective increase in the money supply by debasing the coinage. The silver content of the denarius fell from the time of Augustus, when it was almost pure silver except for some hardening agents, to 0.02 percent by A.D. 268. Following this long period of fiscal and monetary-induced inflation, Emperor Diocletian decided to stop the inflation by his edict of A.D. 301. The penalty for various offenses was death and covered the whole productive process. Naturally the effort

[2]Cf. an amusing article in the *Wall Street Journal,* October 2, 1973.

failed. A comtemporary's comment illustrates some of the effects:

> After the many oppressions which he [Diocletian] put in practice had brought a general dearth upon the empire, he then set himself to regulate the prices of all vendible things. There was much bloodshed upon very slight and trifling accounts; and the people brought provisions no more to markets, since they could not get a reasonable price for them; and this increased the dearth so much that at last after many had died by it, the law itself was laid aside.

Clearly, as this quotation indicates, inflation stimulated by deficit spending is not a new phenomenon, and even absolute control over the private sector of the economy is inadequate to the task of lowering inflation without creating unemployment. If post-World War II governments in Europe and North America have not caused such widespread economic failure in their attempts to "cure" inflation, it is simply because they have not tried hard enough.

Basic micro sources of growth

Since controls do not provide a feasible method for achieving growth without severe strain on the body economic, we might well ask whether a market economy can provide growth without the economy suffering other ills,[3] such as inflation, personal losses of property rights, and so on. The basic determinants of the rates of growth, unemployment, and inflation are found in the individual household, firm, and industry, that is, in the market. How fast the economy can grow and at what cost is determined by the efficiency with which goods and services are produced and distributed, and labor, materials, and capital are used, the ability of the economy to stimulate, incorporate, and develop technological change, and to react quickly to change. Economic efficiency and effective markets are the keystones to growth in economic welfare.

But this proposition is almost a tautology and few economists would disagree with it. The disagreement occurs over

---

[3] We should be aware, however, that growth in a market economy will not necessarily imply a large increase in material goods. Collectively, the individuals in a society may prefer more leisure, less pollution, more personal services, more art, more theater, rather than more physical goods.

whether, if markets are left unimpeded by bureaucracy, they will in practice be efficient. Further, given the obvious deficiencies of existing economies, is the failure one of the market or of bureaucratic controls? And, finally, some would argue that even if markets are efficient, government controls are needed to produce the "good life" and to ensure "income equality."

In the train analogy, most U.K. and U.S. policy decisions can be characterized as devices which impede the efficiency of the train so that one must press ever harder on the accelerator to obtain speed (growth) and then jam on the brakes when the train starts to get completely out of control. This is a major, if not *the* major, cause of so-called business cycles. One would think that those nominally in command would learn by their experience. But they do not. As I have argued extensively, the economic machine is very complicated and without the proper methodology it is too easy for the policy maker to fool himself into believing that what *he* is doing is right while everyone else is wrong. Thus, as long as observers of the economy (like Mr. Hayward above) can refer to isolated statistics in support of highly simplistic notions about how the economy functions, that is, as long as there is discussion void of macroeconomic theory and void of reference to econometric models, then in such an econometric vacuum political persuasion will supplant reasoned argument. The public will learn that a few macro controls like the money supply and fiscal policy are not, nor can they ever be, a cure for the government's failures in micro policies, much less a panacea for economic ills, *only* when hard econometric evidence can be brought to bear on the problem. Even currently, it is possible for government to blame (even sincerely) outside factors beyond its control for the failures of its policies; it can claim without effective refutation that life would have been so much worse without its policies. Only econometric models can be used to settle these disputatious issues, but even that result is some way off in the future.

Motives and misunderstanding in government

I have made numerous criticisms of current government thinking and action. In concluding this paper I shall try to redress the balance by specifying government's roles and indicate positive recommendations in place of negative criticisms. The recommendations reflect my personal views and judgments about what is "beneficial" to society. However, as I have tried to demonstrate, my views are not without support in the economics profession. My opinions have been modified by my own economic research and by my reading of many other economists. My recommendations are not merely a reflection of personal prejudices but are the end result of analysis disciplined by a well-tested theory.

I should emphasize that my criticisms of government policy should in no way be construed as criticisms of the *motives*[4] of politicians and bureaucrats. I certainly do not wish to imply that the general harmful impact of government decision making occurs because government decision makers are greedy, or irresponsible, or do not have the best and most laudable intentions. In truth, the irony is that so much harm is done not because of evil intent but simply because of ignorance or through misunderstanding of economic forces. Less charitably, we must recognize that politicians will act in their own short-term political interest, which often entails a high economic cost to society.[5] And we must also recognize that any change in the political behavior to which both U.K. and U.S. politicians are committed is most unlikely. I quote in support another well-known economist's pragmatic view:

> We should anticipate permanent budget deficits with permanent inflation. It would be highly unrealistic to expect any substantial self-control by Congress to moderate expansion of the budget.... The political process seems inherently unstable and essentially incapable of settling down. The central consequences of political competition are to enlarge and complicate programs, enlarge the government sector and produce increasingly uncertain and erratic rules of the game.[6]

Professor Brunner's remarks apply even more aptly to the United Kingdom.

[4][The irrelevance, and, even worse, the danger, of judging economic policies by motives is discussed and illustrated in Harris and Seldon, *Not from Benevolence...* (London: IEA, Hobart Paper 10, 1977).—ED.]

[5]Gordon Tullock, *The Vote Motive* (London: IEA, Hobart Paper 9, 1976).

[6]Professor Karl Brunner, quoted by Lindley H. Clark, Jr., *Wall Street Journal,* April 12, 1975.

The impossible macro dream

The meritorious idea of using macro-policy instruments to achieve maximum growth with low unemployment, zero inflation, and no other harmful side effects is an impossible dream, given the current state of the macroeconomic art. Even the limited objectives of maximizing growth rates, or alternatively of maintaining for long periods a low unemployment rate through government manipulation of expenditures and the money supply, are simply not possible without the implementation of the required micro policies. The irony is that the implementation of the correct micro policies would probably remove all need for macro policies other than those of maintaining a steady state in the money supply, taxes, and government expenditures.

The only objective which it may be thought can be achieved is short-run stabilization, that is, government use of its macro instruments to counteract *temporary* and essentially *minor* fluctuations in economic activity. But even in this modest role there are dangers. First, there is the temptation to use macro policy instruments on problems, such as the oil embargo, which are essentially micro in nature, and thereby compound our economic difficulties. Secondly, stabilization policies, to be effective, require very sophisticated econometric techniques and very large amounts of highly skilled econometric manpower. No government in Britain (or anywhere else) has been prepared to commit itself to economic engineering by economists *and* to spend the required resources. We are not likely to see for some time an economic NASA, which *might* make short-term stabilization more likely. The result, as far as we can determine from the evidence, is that government policy tends to be destabilizing, rather than stabilizing. The situation is usually saved from deteriorating rapidly by the happy chance that many government actions tend to offset each other's effects. One policy tends to increase aggregate demand, another to decrease it. One policy is inflationary, another is deflationary.

In any event, I shall argue, if government were to pursue actively the required micro policy, I doubt whether we would need any macro stabilization at all. But so long as government is committed to taxing and expenditure and has power over the money supply, it cannot avoid pursuing some policy in these key elements. At best, therefore, that policy should be essentially neutral in all three. The recommendation of such a policy is, and can only be, defended on the knowledge gained from econometric models. Governments have fiscal and monetary controls and they will use them in their own political interest. Thus, the implementation of a policy of neutrality will be accepted by a government only if the electorate is fully aware that such a policy is in its own best interest and votes accordingly.

First, in accord with the recommendations of Professors Milton Friedman and Karl Brunner, and other prominent monetary economists, I suggest that the money supply be increased at a steady rate of about 3 percent per year. To get down to this rate from recent rates in Britain of anything from 10 to 30 percent, I suggest the change be made slowly, not abruptly as usually in monetary policy, such as in the United Kingdom in 1972–73. In monetary management patience is required, a quality in very short supply in government circles because of the political impulse to "take action to 'deal with' " every passing problem. Sudden large changes in the money supply create shocks to the economic system which lead to serious and costly adjustment problems for individuals as well as individual firms because they require time to be able to respond.

Second, in fiscal policy I also suggest neutrality. The government should not only aim at a long-run budget balance, but should slow down, if not reverse, the increase in government expenditures relative to the size of the whole economy. Again patience is the key and changes should be made slowly. I am not arguing for a year-to-year budget balance, nor for a balance for its own sake, nor for misplaced notions of "fiscal solvency." The ever-present tendency which must be checked is for governments to be always at least one step ahead of their tax-financed budgets, to promise benefits without counting the cost.[7] The main objective is to ensure by these means that government policy is stabilizing rather than destabilizing. The stabilizing force comes about because under this policy government expenditures would fall relatively less during a downturn

[7]Analyzed by David R. Morgan, *Over-taxation by Inflation* (London: IEA, Hobart Paper 72, 1977).

in activity (much as happens now) and would *grow* relatively *less* during an upturn.

What are the chances of such neutral policies in practice? Practically nil; at least until the public becomes more completely aware of government's responsibility for past economic ills and that neutrality would prove more efficacious than the attempted cures. An analogy to government macro policy and the public's reaction is the seventeenth century's espousal of bloodletting as a cure for all "ill humors." The practice continued until people started to acquire systematic evidence that the process did not work and to discover procedures which did. At one time, say before World War II, governments could pretend that their policies had little effect on their economies; but not today, not with the percentage of GDP controlled by the British Government rising from 24.2 percent in 1929, 27.8 in 1939, 29.0 in 1948, 42.7 in 1961, to 58.6 percent in 1975. The comparable U.S. figures are 10.0, 14.4, 19.6, 28.7, and 35.3 percent respectively.

These figures, of course, grossly underestimate governmental control of the economy in that much of the control is exercised at the private sector's own direct expense in complying with governmental laws, rules, and regulations. Governments today certainly cannot complain of any lack of power over the private sector, though they may complain about the effectiveness of the power they exercise.

Micro policy—devising property rights

I have indicated at various points in this paper that micro policy has much more potential return to society than macro. Government's micro policy stems from its three crucial roles:

- (*a*) to provide the legal framework, to set the pattern of property rights, to provide the institutional structure within which markets must operate;

- (*b*) to act as policeman, as an arbiter for disputes, and as an agency to enforce the mutual recognition by members of society of one another's property rights;

- (*c*) to oversee the production and distribution of public goods, like national defense, which everyone consumes equally.

(a) The legal framework

Markets work most effectively within an orderly society. Markets are efficient where the costs of acquiring information about market alternatives and when the costs of trading between two or more people are low. Markets are efficient when property rights are easily identified and easily enforced. To provide such conditions for orderly trade is the prime responsibility of government.

But economic life is not static; it is changing continuously. Thus, government has to respond by altering the legal framework and pattern of property rights. In this generation, the problems of water and air pollution have become of great importance in Britain. These are problems essentially of indefinable and not easily enforceable property rights to clean air and fresh water. Laws which codify these rights and facilitate mutual recognition of them would improve market allocation of all resources.

Solutions to problems of the misuse of common resources like the sea are needed with increasing urgency. The current proposal to extend national ownership (i.e., control) of the contents of the sea to 200 miles offshore shows that the way in which fish are caught is a subject of property rights. Off the West coast of the United States the federal authorities, in an attempt to conserve fish, enacted a number of regulations designed to make commercial fishing inefficient by obstructing mechanized techniques, restricting net sizes, hours of fishing, sizes of boats, and so on. Thus, by restricting the efficiency of fishermen, government indirectly tried to legislate conservation of the commercial fish population. Unfortunately, the regulations applied only to U.S. fishermen and not to foreign fishermen in the same waters.

This is one approach. A more efficient method to obtain the "right amount" of fish in response to economic forces would be to assign fishing property rights to designated areas of the sea. The owners of these rights would then find it in their personal self-interest to ensure that the sea areas they controlled were neither over- nor under-fished. The process of catching fish could then become more efficient. The net result would be gains to everyone, including the more inefficient fishermen eliminated by this process, provided they were compensated by those who gained by the change in property rights.

More mundane examples of the government function in keeping property rights up to date are seen in trade relationships, laws of contract, the concept of breach of contract, anticartel and antimonopoly laws, and the legal status, rights, and obligations of trade unions.

Laws on trade unions illustrate the difficulties in changing property rights. When property rights are reassigned someone inevitably loses when others gain. Even when the reassignment means that the gainers (the public) gain more than the losers (the union) lose, the action will seldom, if ever, be taken. This is because the losers are able to bring to bear much stronger *political* pressure than the gainers; unions can organize to create an effective political pressure group which the unorganized consumer and the general public have no chance of combating. Thus, legislation may have to be abandoned for political reasons if those who lose are sufficiently numerous and the expected loss is thought substantial, as in 1969 by a Labour government and virtually in 1972–73 by a Conservative government. There is, however, a solution to what might appear to be a hopeless dilemma. On efficiency grounds the change should not be made unless those who gain stand to gain more than those who lose stand to lose. To effect such a change in property rights, the government must therefore build into the process a method by which those who gain compensate, or "bribe," the losers to accept the change. If the property rights of shop stewards (their political power in the union) are limited in a move to improve economic efficiency, for example, the shop stewards will naturally object strenuously to the proposed change. However, if the incumbents, but *only* the incumbents, can be offered some counterbalancing right, or political power, such as appointing them "inspectors of union policies and procedures" to ensure that the union management itself does not transgress the democratic rights of the union members (a money payment is often not productive because much of the "return" to the shop steward is in his standing and comradeship with the union members), then they can be persuaded to allow the legislation to pass.

Society has clearly gained under this scheme which involves a *voluntary* rearrangement of property rights, for otherwise the voluntary "exchange" would not take place. Further examples are the extraordinary monopoly power of the unionized dock workers in the major ports which not only yields very large returns to the dockers, but also makes the ports highly inefficient; the prevalence of restrictive ("make-work") rules throughout British industry which, while maintaining the continued employment of the *incumbents*, ensures the impoverishment of the rest of the country; and municipal legislation of "standards" for construction, transportation, etc., which legislates the employment in occupations of people who would be more useful to society elsewhere. The spread of such legislation not only lowers the efficiency of the economy, but also raises the level of unemployment at *any* rate of inflation. While it is certainly true that unions are not to blame for inflation, it is equally true that they are directly and indirectly responsible for most of the observed unemployment.

(b) Enforcement of property rights

Even well-defined property rights are of little use unless they can be enforced. There is no gain in declaring theft illegal, if anyone can steal with impunity. Rights have to be enforced or policed. This yields another crucial role for government as the agency best suited usually to perform this task—though private security guards are increasing. The whole apparatus of the courts, the police, the legal and judicial systems, provides the main example. These are all "public goods," or rather assumed to be (economists are not all agreed).

(c) Government and "public goods"

The third role of government is the most controversial: overseeing the production and distribution of public goods. The controversy arises because few goods are purely public and because deciding how much to produce involves big practical difficulties. Further, the extent to which a good is considered to be public, i.e., the extent to which all can use it equally, often (if not always) depends on the way in which it is supplied, and this also is a decision consumers face. For example, crop spraying can be carried out by an airplane so that it can be regarded as a public good (except for the insects, of course); or individuals can spray their own gardens and areas, so that pesticide spraying is now a private good with possibly significant (external) effects on neighbors. Professor Kenneth Goldin has demonstrated[8] that for most, if not all, commodities *traditionally categorized* as public goods, such as national defense, internal security, outdoor recreation, highways, and lighthouses, and so on, society faces a choice between two main methods of distribution, those which enable consumers to have equal access to the good (making it "public"), and those which require selective access, i.e., involve a method of exclusion for nonpurchases of the good (making it "private"). Usually, the former method of distribution is handled by government and the latter is entrusted to the market. But, even in the public goods method of distribution, the market can be used to provide the service and settle the otherwise thorny issue of "how much"; examples are education, toll roads, television, lighthouses[9] (during the early period), research, and even adjudication.

The government dressed in private clothing

The main difficulty is that there is a strong political temptation for government to move more and more into the production of *private* goods, like railways, steel, and so on. The classic justification for government production of what used to be called, misleadingly, "public utilities" (like electricity and gas, for example), was that, since it is technologically inefficient to have more than one firm in the industry, there would be a monopoly. Therefore it was thought to be in the "public interest" that the government should control production. This analysis sounds plausible but is incomplete.

First of all, government-owned monopolies tend to be even more inefficient in production than private monopolies because the threat of entry and the profit incentive to reduce costs and innovate are much weaker. Indeed, governments usually ensure that *their* monopolies are well protected by legal

[8]In "Equal Access vs. Selective Access: A Critique of Public Goods Theory," *Public Choice,* Spring 1977, pp. 53–71.

[9]Besides the previous reference to Professor Goldin, two interesting and delightful references are Professor Ronald H. Coase, "The Lighthouse in Economics," *Journal of Law and Economics* 17 (October 1974), pp. 108–128, and Professor Steven N. S. Cheung, "The Fable of the Bees: An Economic Investigation," *Journal of Law and Economics* 16 (April 1973), pp. 11–33.

constraints on entry (or even potential entry), for example, the U.S. Post Office or British prohibitions on coal imports.[10]

Secondly, allowing private firms to produce, but with government-set maximum "fair rates of return" on capital invested, is not effective either, despite its common occurrence in U.S. electrical utilities. Both theoretical analysis and extensive empirical evidence[11] show that firms operating under such regulations will use capital inefficiently, that costs and prices will be higher and output lower than if they were not regulated at all. In short, this type of regulation is worse than no regulation since *both* the firm and its customers achieve fewer benefits.[12]

Another important example of government creating an inappropriate set of property rights is where it succumbs to the blandishments of industries that want protection from "unfair" competition or from "too much entry" ruining the trade (by lowering prices). In effect, these industries request the government to protect them from the rigors of competition, to do for them what they could not do for themselves—live the quiet but comfortable life of the legally entrenched monopolist.

Sad to say, to suit itself and at high cost to society, government leaps to the supposed rescue of these apparently beleaguered industries. One method is to set up a regulatory commission to raise price, allocate output among the existing firms, and prevent entry. But these are the very actions of a cartel that anticartel and antimonopoly regulation are meant to mitigate. These are the very actions governments claim as the

---

[10][George Tugendhat, *Freedom for Fuel* (London: IEA, Hobart Paper 21, 1963); Colin Robinson, *A Policy for Fuel?* (London: IEA, Occasional Paper 31, 1969); and *Competition for Fuel* (Supplement), IEA, 1971.—ED.]

[11]An introduction to the theoretical and empirical literature is: Professors H. Averch and L. Johnson, "Behavior of the Firm Under Regulatory Constraint," *American Economic Review,* December 1962, pp. 1053–1069; Professors E. Bailey and J. Malone, "Resource Allocation and the Regulated Firm," *The Bell Journal of Economics and Management Science* 1, no. 1 (1970), pp. 129–142; and H. Petersen, "The Effect of Regulation on Production Costs and Output Prices in the Private Electrical Utility Industry" (Memorandum No. 151, Center for Research in Economic Growth, Stanford University, 1973). [Ivy Papps, *Government and Enterprise* (London: IEA, Hobart Paper 61, 1975), also discusses these issues.—ED.]

[12]George J. Stigler, *The Citizen and the State* (Chicago: University of Chicago Press, 1975).

reason for nationalization. Consider railways in both the United States and United Kingdom: In the United States regulation, and in the United Kingdom nationalization, were unnecessary.

The same protective effect is achieved by government passing the required legislation but without the costs of a "regulatory commission," that is, by a governmentally enforced cartel, but without calling it what it is. When these contrivances are put in this stark form, stripped of the obfuscation provided by official governmental language, they seem too incredible to be true, but they are. Except by government legislation, how else could U.S. farmers producing, for example, lemons, tobacco, milk, cotton, peanuts, rice, corn, etc., etc., or British producers of milk, etc., obtain the benefits of a cartel without the costs? How else could highly inefficient small-scale producers be perpetuated for decades?

My questions are not rhetorical because there is another method, a favorite of all governments, including Britain's Labour and Conservative parties. The government can guarantee to buy the product at a high price, subsidize the industry, lend it money (with little expectation of having it repaid), or force the industry's customers to buy the firm's products—through "buy British" legislation, use of nationalized industries such as coal and steel to buy from inefficient high-cost suppliers, tariffs, import quotas, straight subsidies, and so on.

One of the ostensible reasons for these highly inefficient actions is the desire to prevent unemployment in an industry like coal or cars, or in a geographic region like Glasgow or Coventry. Praiseworthy as the objective may seem, the action is shortsighted because it perpetuates rather than mitigates the problem.[13] Industries which are declining are declining for very good reasons: They are inefficient or are producing a less useful product than their competitors. Labor, land, materials, energy, buildings, and other resources should be moving out of them and into growing industries. This is particularly important for labor. If labor moves out of declining and into growing

[13]Graham Hallett, Peter Randall, and E. G. West, *Regional Policy for Ever?* (London: IEA Readings No. 11, 1973).

industries, we are all better off, including the people who would otherwise have stayed in the declining industry. There are costs to moving and gaining new skills,[14] but government's response should be to lower these costs and encourage the move, not hinder it. Skilled labor is a valuable resource, and it will not be wasted in a competitive market. If shipbuilding declines, oil rigs take their place. If the demand for book-keepers and clerks declines, the demand for computer operators, programmers, and keypunchers increases. If the demand for government employees declines, there is an ever-increasing demand for their services in the private sector.

The required functions of government

To conclude, government does have a vital function: to foster and to protect competitive markets so that the economy can grow efficiently and in accord with the multitudinous interests of its members. Government should see that the economic game is played vigorously and according to the rules. But the referee cannot also play, for who then will referee the referee?

---

[14]The difficulty in obtaining housing in a new town is a good example of a cost of moving, especially if electrician Smith has to go to the bottom of the queue for a council house. In terms of retraining, the "burden" falls mainly on the young, those who are deciding where to work and what to do, and those who have the best alternative opportunities. Industries do not die overnight and, at least without governmental interference, people would adjust themselves to slowly changing demands for their services. Those who claim it is "unfair" to encourage people to move from Welsh coal towns, for example, where "they have always lived," do not seem to know that many of these towns were created less than a century ago by the lure of coal mining.

6. Summary and Recommendations

A. SUMMARY OF THE ARGUMENT

Economics is a *stochastic* science. We can only talk about the *odds* in favor of or against an economic event taking place. We can *never* say in economics that something *will* happen; we can merely give the *probability* of its *occurrence*, i.e., say how *likely* it is. Economic relationships between variables are said to be stochastic in the sense that, given the values for one set of *conditioning* (or exogenous) variables, we can determine the probabilities of occurrence for the remaining *dependent* (or endogenous) variables. Economic theory shows how to relate conditioning variables, which are usually determined by noneconomic forces, to dependent variables, which are determined by the economic relationships.

Econometrics is the bridge between theory and real life. Econometrics, a judicious blend of economic theory, statistical theory, and mathematics, is the tool which:
— reformulates loose theoretical statements into precise empirically relevant statements;
— *"tests"* economic theories, that is, enables us to reject inadequate theories which do not explain what we observe;
— enables us to apply economic theory to practical problems and answer relevant policy questions.

One of the most important practical lessons to be learned from econometrics is to recognize the problem of *identification*, the problem of how to disentangle *apparent* cause from cause from consequence. Econometrics shows the need to examine *all* the relevant data, not only those items which support one's preconceived notions. The political practice of citing only agreeable statistics can never settle economic arguments, whereas the econometric approach of examining all the data and weighing them carefully in the context of rigorous theory can.

Econometric *forecasts* are answers to "What if?" questions. A forecast is a statement about the odds in favor of a value of the dependent variable given the values of the conditioning variables; a forecast is merely a statement about relationships between economic variables. Economic events *cannot* be *predicted*, since one cannot give the odds in favor of the conditioning events occurring. Thus, while economists cannot "foresee" the future, they can understand it. No one else can predict the future; but neither can he understand it.

*Micro*economics deals with the relationships between individuals and firms and between unions and government agencies; with markets and the decisons of individuals both within markets and within collective organizations like governments, bureaucracies, and even committees. *Macro*economics deals with the relationships between broad aggregates defined over an entire region or economy such as total consumption, investment, wealth, and income. These variables are measured by *index* numbers. They provide a useful measure of the aggregates only when the *proportions* of the individual items which make up the aggregate remain the same. Micro theory enables us to understand the relationships which underlie the macro relationships.

Econometric procedures can be used to obtain forecasts, i.e., statements about probabilites of occurrence of the endogenous macro variables given the conditioning variables. Thus, the econometric macro model can be tested and, if not rejected, applied to practical policy problems.

The methods of "predicting" or rather attempting to predict macro variables which are used are naïve prediction and ad hoc construction models. The former assume essentially that the past will repeat itself so that past observations can be projected into the future. Little, if any, economic theory is used in obtaining these "predictions." Ad hoc construction uses a modeler's hunches, feelings, and intuitive insights to modify results obtained by either of the above methods so that the resulting prediction meets with the modeler's preconceived notions.

The advantage of econometric models is that they provide a method for learning from past mistakes in a scientific manner, that is, one has objective criteria for evaluating the model which can be tested and rejected. Naïve prediction models and, a fortiori, ad hoc models do not have this advantage. Econometric models have the disadvantage that learning from them can proceed only as fast as economic theory grows, and in the current state of the art can be used to provide only partial answers to a few policy questions. In contrast, naïve and ad hoc models can always be used to produce some prediction, on *any* variable, even if one can have little confidence in the prediction, and even if one cannot judge how likely one is to be wrong. But if a modeler is asked today to produce a prediction —say, inventory levels in 1979—he can quickly cite a figure; whereas the econometric modeler may not be able to say anything other than to express his ignorance.

Macro models used for policy in Britain and the United States, as opposed to models used purely for research purposes, combine all three approaches in varying degrees because the demand by policy users is for predictions, not forecasts, for numbers and percentages, no matter how obtained.

Practical lessons of macro models

A few of the practical lessons learned primarily from the use of econometric macro models over the last twenty-five years are:

(a) —Rejection:

(i) of those notions of Galbraith which have been formalized and subjected to test;

(ii) of the early simple versions of monetarism;

(iii) of the Keynesian explanation of the 1930s depression;

(iv) of all the early simple notions of multiplier effects and elementary Keynesianism;

(v) of aggregate demand as the *sole* driving force in market economics; the importance of supply is now realized to have been seriously underplayed;

(vi) of the ubiquitous usefulness of *static* models;

(vii) of the supposed efficacy of dealing only with broad macro aggregates;

(viii) of the Phillips curve and stimulation of research on the operation of labor markets.

(b)—Recognition:

(i) of the role of government action in increasing general uncertainty and in destabilizing the economy;

(ii) of the role of government in changing general economic efficiency through changes in property rights;

(iii) of the importance of the money supply, financial institutions, and the financial actions of both locals and national governments.

B. RECOMMENDATIONS FOR POLICY

These lessons would seem to imply the following policy recommendations for government action:

1. Take a "neutral" position on fiscal and monetary policy.
2. Develop and enforce personal property rights.
3. Enact measures and repeal old laws to facilitate the smooth operation of the market economy.
4. Encourage private and individual *versus* central and "collective" decision making.

Economists have much to learn, but through econometrics they have learned some lessons and will learn many more. Who else will?

A Skeptical View of Forecasting in Britain

Ralph Harris

It may be thought that the only definite way of establishing the case for skepticism on conventional macro models as a guide for "management" of the economy would be to take them apart and show where the postulated categories, correlations, and coefficients are wrong. That would imply that I (or others known to me) knew the correct answers and could build a better (if not perfect) model. But even the "experts" have shown they are not competent to discharge that task. Indeed, a strong critique could be based on the very broad empirical evidence in Britain that successive generations of macro models have proved a dismal failure in guiding economic policy.

It is some years since Mr. Christopher Dow's devastating demonstration that postwar "stabilization policy" had been destabilizing because both timing and "correction" tended to be perverse.[1] Macro-model-mongers may plead in defense that government objectives after 1945 were inconsistent: full employment, fixed exchange rate, stable prices, open economy, low interest rates, and the rest. By the late 1950s, however, the familiar "stop-go" oscillations led to a more single-minded emphasis on "growth" under the National Economic Development Council. Instead of avoiding instability, the macro forecasters from the National Institute of Economic and Social Research (NIESR), the Cambridge Social Accounting Matrix (SAM), and the Treasury contributed to even wider fluctuations between booms and slumps in the 1960s, with intensifying inflation and unemployment, but without the prized goal of higher (let alone sustained) growth. And since 1972, when the supposed constraint of a fixed exchange rate was abandoned,

---

[1] J. C. R. Dow, *The Management of the British Economy 1945-60* (Cambridge: At the University Press, National Institute of Economic & Social Research Economic & Social Studies: No. 22, 1970).

the economy has been even more severely mismanaged. But the macro meddlers are not so easily defeated: If their models have proved no good, they simply conclude we must build bigger or better models.

Pretense of knowledge

So I turn to the more fundamental, a priori objections. My case against the model manipulators rests on the solid foundation of *ignorance*, not only mine, freely confessed, but even more the ignorance of the modelers which is all the more dangerous if they lack humility—as has been known among economists at the NIESR and Treasury. Indeed, all confident claims to comprehensive knowledge are a sham. Their "sophistication" borders on naïveté. Macro models may be the most prestigious branch of modern economics technically (or rather pyrotechnically), but we should be on guard. "Prestigious" is derived from "prestidigitator," which according to the Shorter Oxford English Dictionary is concerned with conjuring, juggling, sorcery, and, I must report, cheating...

In short, the claim of some model makers to produce a computable matrix to help steer short-term economic policy is founded on a *pretense to knowledge* which they do not have, the pretense that Professor F. A. Hayek[2] has criticized as based on a confusion between the natural and social sciences. The model-mongers fly in the face of Pigou's warning against "the mere building of cheap toys"[3]—except that their crude statistical "meccano" sets are no longer cheap.

Analysis of the perfectionist requirements of the modelers cuts the ground from under their feet. Among the minimum requirements for an operational "model" of the British economy are that some supereconomists can identify the significant variables, distinguish the exogenous from the endogenous, put appropriate numbers to them—in percentages, indices, pounds (current and constant), absolute magnitudes—and then link the resulting mixture of estimates and out-turns together in correct causal sequence that will transmit the effects of stipulated (and

[2]F. A. Hayek, *Full Employment at Any Price?* (London: IEA, Occasional Paper 45, 1975).

[3]"An Economist's Apologia," in A. C. Pigou, *Economics in Practice* (1936; reprint ed., Westport, Conn.: Hyperion, 1978).

often simultaneous) change to all the components to be predicted. All this implies *comprehensive* knowledge of physical and monetary correlations, coefficients of production, elasticities of demand and supply, marginal rates of substitution, import contents of changes in output... It would require a sustained achievement of a *uniformly* high standard of *accurate* estimation that may one day be possible but is certainly far beyond our present reach.

As with a moonshot, it would not suffice to get some bits more or less right. The ability to *hit* the target and not shoot off into space depends on the *weakest* link in the sequence of analysis and measurement. Yet, as two Nobel laureates of recent years—Hayek[4] in 1974, Friedman[5] in 1976—have insisted, prediction in the *social* sciences is poles apart from prediction in the *physical* sciences. Prediction in the natural sciences relies on understanding the interplay of relatively few variables and eliminating extraneous influences—almost in pure laboaratory conditions. In sharp contrast, a comprehensive theory in the social sciences must take account of very large numbers of *particular* facts which are so widely diffused that—even if they are not perpetually changing—knowledge of them could never be brought together at the center.

Corporate forecasting and national planning

Much confusion is caused by failure to understand the difference between corporate forecasting and national planning. Some years ago Professor Oskar Lange, the influential Polish economist who believed that markets were not only essential but could be built into socialism, said rather too confidently in criticism of Professors Hayek and Lionel Robbins: "Let us put the simultaneous equations on an electronic computer and we shall obtain a solution in less than a second." "...the electronic computer," he added, "does not replace the market. It fulfils a function which the market was never able to perform."[6]

[4]Hayek, *Full Employment at Any Price?*

[5]Milton Friedman, *Inflation and Unemployment: The New Dimension of Politics* (the 1976 Nobel Memorial Lecture) (London: IEA, Occasional Paper 51, 1977).

[6]Oskar Lange, "The Computer and the Market," in C. Feinstein (ed.),

Sir Frank McFadzean, until recently chairman of Shell and therefore no stranger to corporate planning, now chairman of British Airways, and visiting professor of economics at Strathclyde, referred some years ago in his polemic *Galbraith and the Planners*[7] to the ten million Soviet citizens who, in the absence of spontaneous market mechanisms, were estimated in the 1960s to be engaged in the manual collection and processing of data. Academician Glushkov, he added, warned that if Russia attempted to simulate the detailed operation of the Russian economy, it would require "several quintillion relationships to be examined and appraised" and that would take several years even with "a million computers processing 30,000 operations a second."

A disillusioned special adviser to the chancellor recently likened the Treasury's "vast economic model" to "a coral reef in its uncontrolled growth.... It has reached a point where no single individual can grasp its complexities."[8] Alas, or perhaps we should say thank goodness, there is no escape for modelers in computers that would undoubtedly tempt power-hungry politicians—or even economists—to create a human beehive before 1984. The macro forecasters are technical tyros with a larger capability to intensify rather than remedy the confusions into which they have helped bring economic policy by 1977. In contrast, a competent businessman operating in competitive markets soon learns that his forward plans are beset by uncertainty, and he has a strong motive to revise all forecasts as their always tentative extrapolations look like being falsified by changing reality.

Equilibrium or rogue elephant?

A problem that confronts all model builders is whether they regard their starting point as some variant of equilibrium or claim to know the equilibrium point toward which current tendencies in the economy are propelling us. Or do they reject the concept of equilibrium and suppose the system is inherently

---

Capitalism, Socialism and Economic Growth (Cambridge: At the University Press, 1967).

[7]Frank McFadzean, *Galbraith and the Planners* (Strathclyde, Scotland: Strathclyde University Press, 1968).

[8]Adrian Ham, *Financial Times,* August 5, 1976.

and incorrigibly unstable in the absence of perpetual discretionary intervention? By simple analogy, should "the economy" be regarded as an ecological system with an underlying balance that is constantly trying to assert itself despite changes from outside the system? Or is it a *mechanism* that will run off the lines unless politicians are constantly winding it up, changing the regulator, and switching the points?

Reality of ignorance

Three a priori postulates should prompt suspicions against even the most heavily qualified claims of comprehensive models as a guide to economic policy.

(i) *Ignorance of the present*

The rival theories of economists reveal no agreement between the professionals about the operation of the economy or the leading processes of economic causation. We have left behind the glad, confident morning of Keynesian consensus which opened the door to the macro-mongers. We are no longer sure about the underlying determinants of employment or real income, the role of investment or the effects of a budget deficit, the significance of monetary aggregates, and so much more. It is not surprising that the predictions of rival models differ randomly and the computer printouts always need what Professor Lawrence Klein, President Carter's economic adviser, describes privately as "tender, loving care" before being displayed to the waiting world. What confidence can we have in this impressive rigmarole, if the resulting figures have to be "loved" to make them plausible?

(ii) *Uncertainty of the future*

Except in a closed, static system, an economy is characterized by *pervasive* change and uncertainty. There are not only the perpetual jolts imparted by ceaseless and often arbitrary, or even irrational, political changes both at home and abroad. There is also the unfathomable, immeasurable, imponderable "confidence," or lack of it, which may exert a decisive influence over developments that swamp the *measurable* or material changes that can be fed into computers. Above all, there are changes in resources, techniques, raw materials, synthetic products, demand, fashion, foreign trade, that have between them totally transformed the inputs and outputs of whole industries and sectors of the economy throughout the postwar period.

There are of course patterns, uniformities, and regularities which can be handled by extrapolations. But that does not help enough. All that is most important for economic development comes from the discontinuities which *cannot be known until they happen.* The best way of dramatizing the disruptions caused by such unforeseeable changes is perhaps to recall some of the more confident forecasts that have mocked the pretentions of would-be planners (in government *and business*) throughout the postwar years. It is painful now to recall the miscalculations and improbabilities of some of the most expert forecasters:

— the famous postwar fuel shortage that never emerged until the Arabs took everyone by surprise with the oil price;
— the miracle of nuclear energy that was to solve the fuel shortage that never happened;
— the manpower budgeting that invented shortages of skills no longer even remembered, ending up with the bizarre "manpower gap" of the National Plan;
— the complacency over the supply of doctors that missed the large-scale exodus of a large proportion of the products of our medical schools and made us dependent upon immigrants more urgently needed in their own lands;
— the supposed decline in medical costs when the NHS reduced disease;
— the phantom shortage of steel-making capacity that haunted the NEDC, the National Plan, Sir Robert Shone—and everyone except Sir Monty Finniston;
— the "world dollar shortage" proclaimed by Sir Donald MacDougall just as the world was to be overwhelmed by the flood;
— the electricity shortage that never was, but that led to massive centralized misinvestment in peak capacity which remained idle;
— the sacrosanctity of fixed exchange rates, the projected growth rates of successive national plans, those oft-heralded but so elusive balance-of-payments surpluses...

Many of these forecasts looked highly impressive at the time of their conception. Some economists were as badly caught out as politicians—perhaps because they tend to look for regularities and continuities: "the many in the one" rather than Marshall's "the one in the many."[9] The costs were not borne by the model makers, who indeed built good jobs and reputations on them, but by the people who suffered, through lack of doctors, overinvestment, increased prices, higher taxation.

Statistical analysis and speculation are useful, but only *within the discipline and information of markets*. Then they can enable us to judge the *direction* of possible future changes— and sometimes their order of magnitude. But the best results are achieved by specialists, usually in relatively small sectors, who have learned how to blend detailed particular knowledge with a good "feel" for those immeasurable forces—that comes only from familiarity with micro knowledge that is the fruit of markets but that, by definition, must be left out of the reckoning by the "scientific" macro statistician.

All economic forecasting is guesswork—and never more beguiling than when churned out to three decimal places[10] by computers, wired up to Heath-Robinson contraptions, fed on a comparative spoonful of stale semistatistics, claiming to simulate the working of a complex open economy. Even if we regard the economy as stable—with an in-built tendency to adjust itself toward an equilibrium state—the future will be different from the past in ways we cannot know in advance.

All forecasting starts from the present—or more strictly from the latest uncorrected time-series or census. It must therefore depend on some variant of extrapolating variables from the past into the future with whatever adjustments are thought appropriate in differential rates of change operating on them. Thus all forecasting is in an important sense *backward*-looking—vividly compared to steering a ship by its wake. It is the very opposite from the impression of *prescience* conveyed, not always innocently, by modelers.

However good measurements, correlations, techniques be-

[9]Letter to Professor A. L. Bowley reproduced in A. C. Pigou (ed.), *Memorials of Alfred Marshall* (Macmillan, 1925), p. 421.

[10]Marshall warned Bowley (ibid.) against putting "the varnish of mathematical accuracy to many places of decimals on results the premises of which are not established within 20 or 50 percent...."

come, the picture of the future will remain obscured by the element of "uncertainty" which Frank Knight distinguished from mere "risk."[11] *Risks* present the statistician (or actuary) with little anxiety of being proved wrong because they relate to recurrent variations—in weather, familiar diseases, death rates, and other hazards—which can be grouped together over large numbers of cases or over cycles, assessed by well-known probabilities, and offset by the equivalent of an insurance premium. In contrast, *uncertainty* relates to the equity element for which classical economic theory provided the residual reward of profit or penalty of loss. It refers to unique, discontinuous changes in demand, innovation, discovery, which cannot be absorbed by probability theory.

The merit of a competitive market is that it is in principle (if not always in practice) capable of adapting supply and demand promptly to the impact of uncertainty through changes in relative prices, which induce scattered consumers and producers to adjust their actions—even without knowing the source of the disturbance to their previous calculations. It is, in this sense, the optimum discovery procedure in a changing world of imperfect human foresight confronting sparse resources.

(iii) *The macro mirage*

A third weakness undermines the facile assumptions on which ambitious models rest. Nonmarket economists (along with many others) fall into the well-baited trap of oversimplifying the much more complex phenomena of the so-called social sciences into far fewer categories than the inherently simpler physical sciences acknowledge. Scientists proper are able to distinguish all matter in terms of a finite number of elements objectively defined by their constant atomic and molecular composition. (In the real world mathematicians acknowledge that even theirs is an approximate science.) Economists have no such capability, yet some of them do not hesitate to claim scientific validity for crude theories about the effect of changing quantities of such ragbag macro categories as "investment," "manufacturing output," "employment," "exports." The macro men alight on the concept of "capital" and think that,

11Frank Knight, *Risk, Uncertainty and Profit* (1921; reprint ed., Chicago: University of Chicago Press, 1971).

because they can put a number to it, they are handling a concrete entity which can be linked with index numbers over a time series to predict changes in other macro concepts—"output" and such-like bundles of dissimilarities.

What distinguishes a "capital" from a "consumer" good is often not its *physical* characteristics but the *economic* way it is used. Some education is investment (in improved skills that can be marketed) and some is pure, direct consumption and enjoyment of skills or knowledge. A similar duality applies to private cars or domestic equipment, like washing machines, which are capital goods masquerading as ("durable") consumer goods and which yield an income in kind over a long period.

Yet the short-lived 1965–66 National Plan, taking its cue from Mr. Andrew Shonfield's fashionable but in effect mischievous Penguin, *Economic Policy since the War*, relied on increased capital investment to raise the growth rate via the magical "capital-output ratio." This ignores the microeconomic truth that identical capital equipment may be more or less efficiently employed according to the varying pressures of competition, as influenced by trade unions, foreign trade, nationalized monopoly.

The same distinction between the technical and the economic applies to such crude macro concepts as "fuel," "transport," "employment"—even disaggregated into regions, sex, age groups, trades... However much this macro make-believe is chopped up into subcategories, the results are not refined substances nor necessarily even cohesive groups but still monstrous heterogeneous heaps, all on their devious ways to creating a myriad kaleidoscope of ever-changing goods, services, satisfactions, for the ultimate, unknown consumers at home and abroad.[12]

Scientism and statistics

The fallacies to which I have drawn attention stem from what Hayek has called "scientism," which can be summarized as the misapplication of the procedures of the physical sciences to the very different world of the social sciences. Economic laws are "statements of general tendencies" with the ubi-

[12]The reader is referred to the writings of Professors L. M. Lachmann and G. L. S. Shackle on these economic fundamentals.

quitous qualification that "other things remain equal"—which they *never* do.

I do not enter a blanket condemnation of mathematics, which was used effectively by Marshall, Keynes, and Edgeworth. It is true that econometric analysis and algebraic formulations can often throw up valuable insights which can then be expressed for laymen in perfectly straightforward language. But, as Keynes said of Marshall, he used "much self-obliteration" to keep diagrammatic methods "in their proper place"—which was usually in footnotes or appendices.[13] Marshall in turn reviewed Edgeworth's *Mathematical Psychics:*

> It will be interesting to see how far he succeeds in preventing his mathematics from running away with him, and carrying him out of sight of the actual facts of economics.[14]

A century later "self-obliteration" is hardly the style of the present-day macro modelers. Their occasional reservations and qualifications are usually lost to the politicians who see only clear, concise, comforting statistics. Yet the mathematics the modelers proudly flourish would be regarded by competent practitioners as "dog maths" on a par with what schoolboys used to know as "dog Latin."

Alas, despite these warnings of the inherent limitations of mathematics, its modern exponents have been tempted by the advance in computer technology into believing that improvements in the hardware and software will compensate for the *incurable* deficiencies of the statistical inputs.

Proof of the pudding...

Enthusiasts for macro forecasting should be required to study the assessment of the results of various models J. C. K. Ash and D. J. Smyth summarized in *Bankers Magazine* (October 1973) under the intriguing title "Who forecasts the British economy best?" Among their findings from examining the efforts of the Treasury, NIESR, OECD, *Sunday Times,* and *Sunday Telegraph* between 1967 and 1971 were the following gems:

1. All the half-yearly forecasts of the GDP and its main components exhibited large variations of error and were fre-

[13]*Memorials of Alfred Marshall*, p. 25.
[14]Ibid., p. 26.

quently more wide of the mark than a blind prediction of "no change."

2. The *Sunday Telegraph*, relying on less sophistication and more hunch by business economists accustomed to the flavor of markets, did better throughout than the elaborate econometric models.

3. Measured by Theil's inequality coefficient, the largest error by all five forecasters of the nine components of GDP was in the Treasury's forecast of public authority current spending. The coefficient was 1.42 where an accurate forecast would have yielded a coefficient of zero, and a forecast of "no change" would have shown up as 1.0.

4. Although the NIESR returned the best scores for some periods and some components, and the OECD or Treasury scored better for others, none was *consistently* good over the range (except the *Sunday Telegraph*).

5. Leaving aside the range of error and turning to the half-yearly forecasts of the direction of change (i.e., the plus or minus sign), Ash and Smyth found that (apart from the *Sunday Telegraph*) the best, or least bad, performance was by the NIESR: "about a *quarter* of all the turning points are missed, and about a quarter of its turning points are *spurious*." In other words, the best (least worst) forecaster half the time simply got the *sign* wrong!

6. In the ranking of "best buy," the *Sunday Telegraph* was the only supplier whose forecasts were all rated "acceptable" (except for stockbuilding). Others were inconsistently good for some and bad for others. Of the Treasury's forecast of public authority spending, Ash and Smyth concluded with the damning verdict: "unacceptable and not safe in any use."

In April 1975, the persistent Mr. Ash returned to the fray,[15] this time concentrating on the Treasury forecasts from 1968 to 1974. He found it had slightly reduced the error in public spending, but had increased it in the key variable of GDP where the inequality coefficient hovered around the dreaded figure of 1.0 that would have resulted from simply assuming "no change"!

[15] J. C. K. Ash, "Forecasting the Forecasters," *Bankers Magazine,* April 1975.

As evidence that the pertinacious Mr. Ash may not be above suspicion, he indulges in an exercise of "retrospective forecasting" to show that an equation can be derived which, if applied to all forecasts, would have given a better result—on average by about 5 percent. But he does not venture to say whether he thinks *backward* "correction" would hold for *future* discrepancies between forecasts and out-turns.

The bigger the worse

What emerges from this rather uninhibited demolition of the claims of macro modelers? I am not arguing against the use of mathematics and formal econometric models for exploring or testing possible correlations between significant variables within a closed or limited circuit. Sectoral models of the market for labor, or more specifically for shipping, tourism, or economic textbooks, may advance our understanding and improve the quality of competitive *business* decisions where errors are penalized by *losses*.

But the more widely we try to extend the catchment area to construct a comprehensive model of the economy as a whole, the more tenuous the calculations are bound to become. To quote Hayek on the more realistic founders of mathematical economics:

> Their systems of equations describing the pattern of a market equilibrium are so framed that, *if* we were able to fill in *all* the blanks of the abstract formulae, that is, *if* we knew all the parameters of these equations, we could calculate the prices and quantities of all commodities and services sold.[16]

But, as Vilfredo Pareto clearly stated, its purpose cannot be "to arrive at a numerical calculation of prices," since to assume we could ascertain the data was, in Pareto's word, "absurd."[17]

The real danger is that "the pretense of knowledge" will lead governments to believe they can control the economy more extensively and to finer margins of error than are attainable—with contrary, destabilizing consequences. And as the results of

[16]Hayek, *Full Employment at Any Price?* p. 35.
[17]Quoted by Hayek, *Full Employment at Any Price?*, p. 35, from Pareto's *Manuel d'économie politique* (Paris, 1927).

past mistakes are manifest and multiplied, the politicians will be tempted into still wider and wider demonstrations of their incompetence—stemming above all from their irremediable, collective ignorance of the necessary data and relationships.

Alternative approach

What is the discipline on the overuse of models in government? What can be done about it? and, Are these models necessary? My answers must be "None," "Nothing," and "No." As a guide to the general management of the economy they remain a snare and a delusion.

The alternative approach is derived from my original postulates of ignorance and uncertainty. The only mechanism—or organism[18]—that can engage dispersed knowledge and differing forecasts into an operational communications network as a guide for action is the competitive market. High priority should, therefore, be given to reforms that will remove avoidable obstacles to its freer functioning.

Markets are like a whole series of linked computers into which are fed daily information and estimates about the changing ingredients of supply and demand, and out of which pour a ceaseless feedback of signals mostly in the form of changing relative prices that guide producers and consumers in adapting to change. Markets not only use more—and more accurate—information than the most complex model conceivable; they provide *incentives* for individuals to take appropriate action as producers and consumers—disaggregated down to hundreds of thousands of separable and specific resources, goods, and services.

Since unavoidable "uncertainty" arises from changes that can never be accurately foreseen, competition brings the advantage of a spread of rival forecasting estimates. Companies that are proved most wrong will have strong financial inducements to follow their most successful competitors. Corporate plans may extend five or ten years forward but they are daily subject to revision in the light of changing market indicators.

[18]In an essay entitled "Mechanical and Biological Analogies in Economics," Alfred Marshall concluded "in the more advanced stages of economics" that "the Mecca of the economist is economic biology rather than economic dynamics." (*Memorials of Alfred Marshall,* p. 318.)

How perfect?

To those who respond with the trite catchphrase that "markets are imperfect," there are three answers. First, those who seek perfection are not really of this world. Nirvana comparison with perfect but unreal forms of government machinery is futile. Second, markets are far less imperfect than the ad hoc sequence of discretionary intervention by politicians—guided by a mixture of scientific-seeming models, arbitrary party passions, and ever-present electoral calculations. The real pathology of planners is seen in the politician's craving for certainty —which is doomed to disappointment as successive efforts to impose "stable growth" have plunged us all into deeper and darker uncertainties.

The third answer to people obsessed with the "imperfections" of markets is that the worst are man-made and can be removed or at least reduced by man. How can we be impressed by political rhetoric about the "failure" of the market system when government has come to control 60 percent of the national income, financed by highly distortionary taxes and subsidies, and has destroyed most of the market instrumentation by pervasive controls over prices—including wages, rents, profits?

How stable?

A more justified anxiety is whether, if markets *were* allowed to work, the resulting total outcome would be stable—would tend toward a tolerable equilibrium? As a self-confessed, half-baked Keynesian coming down from Cambridge after the war, I would have replied: "No, not in the absence of active demand management—and all that. . ." But, working at the Institute of Economic Affairs since 1957, I have been increasingly impressed by the monetarist school which has now amassed compelling evidence that the worst instabilities of economic systems, down the centuries and across the world, have been caused by the mismanagement by governments of the money supply. Having watched their disruptive record in Britain over the past decade, I have marveled that the residual market mechanisms have performed so well in keeping the show on the road: At least the daily (private) bread and milk gets delivered—if the daily (government) post does not!

The case for reconstructing the market as the best available

computer would start with the reasons for the Keynesian revolution which lie in the massive unemployment between the
wars. Its cause was thought to be a chronic, inbuilt deficiency
in aggregate demand—but it can be explained by a world-wide
contraction in the money supply.[19] The depression was aggravated in Britain by adherence to an overvalued (i.e., non
market) exchange rate, and by the resulting protectionist-pres-
ervationist policies pursued by Tory and National governments.

It remains true that in the absence of Keynesian management, unemployment might stand higher than we would wish.
That level is largely determined by exogenous *real* factors in the
labor market,[20] including obstacles to geographical and occupa-
tional mobility of labor and aggravated by untaxed social security benefits which increase voluntary unemployment and
lengthen the search time for new jobs.

If Keynesian expansionist policy is used to drive unemployment below this "natural" or sustainable rate, the gain is
short-term and purchased at the expense of accelerating inflation. As inflationary expectations are alerted and escalate, it requires ever-larger injections of purchasing power to achieve a
dwindling effect on employment—until galloping inflation and
mounting unemployment stare us in the face.[21]

The record was set forth by William Rees-Mogg in the
Times.[22] The plot of M3 (1965–73) against the price index
(1967–75) provides powerful reason to suppose that the abate-
ment of inflation during early 1976 had nothing much to do
with price controls, but followed—after the customary lag of
about two years—the cutback by the Labour chancellor, Mr.
Healey, in the rate of growth in money supply.

Within a stable monetary environment, the more freely
markets are permitted to operate, the more responsive the

---

[19]Milton Friedman, *The Counter-Revolution in Monetary Theory* (London:
IEA, Occasional Paper 33, 1970).

[20]Friedman, *Unemployment versus Inflation?,* especially the British commentary by David Laidler.

[21]Hayek, *Full Employment at Any Price?*

[22]William Rees-Mogg, the (London) *Times,* July 13, 1976; the article was
somewhat dogmatically entitled "How a 9.4% Excess Money Supply Gave Britain a 9.4% Inflation."

economy will be to those inevitable uncertainties arising from nonmonetary factors that can neither be foreseen nor exorcised by forecasting models. With Sam Brittan, Milton Friedman, Peter Jay, A. A. Walters, and a swelling army of leading economists, I would therefore argue against macro models as a guide to fine tuning and for reliance instead on a fixed, announced monetary rule as the best guarantee of the optimum stability available to us.

I do not propose to fall into the trap of forecasting that forecasting will *never* be made adequate by improved techniques of control or monitoring of variables or identification of nonuniformities. But that is not a necessary part of my case. I have to maintain only that such techniques have *not yet* been devised. Until that day we must not suppose that they have. And until that day, which may be decades or centuries away, the market is the best computer/model we have. Let us use it and be grateful.

RECOMMENDED READING

Becker, Gary S. *The Economic Approach to Human Behavior.* Chicago: University of Chicago Press, 1976.

Boulding, Kenneth E. *Economics as a Science.* New York: McGraw-Hill, 1970.

Buchanan, James M. "Is Economics the Science of Choice?" In *Roads to Freedom: Essays in Honor of F. A. Hayek,* edited by Erich Streissler, pp. 47–64. London: Routledge & Kegan Paul, 1969.

Dolan, Edwin G., ed. *The Foundations of Modern Austrian Economics.* Menlo Park, Calif.: Institute for Humane Studies, 1976.

Egger, John B. "The Austrian Method." In *New Directions in Austrian Economics,* edited by Louis M. Spadaro. Kansas City: Sheed Andrews and McMeel, 1978.

Friedman, Milton. *Essays in Positive Economics.* Chicago: University of Chicago Press, 1953.

Hayek, F. A. *The Counter-Revolution of Science.* Chicago: University of Chicago Press, 1952.

————. *New Studies in Philosophy, Politics, and Economics.* Chicago: University of Chicago Press, 1978.

Ischboldin, Boris. "A Critique of Econometrics." *Review of Social Economy* 18 (September 1960).

Kauder, Emil. *A History of Marginal Utility Theory.* Princeton, N.J.: Princeton University Press, 1965.

Kirzner, Israel. *Competition and Entrepreneurship.* Chicago: University of Chicago Press, 1974.

————. *The Economic Point of View.* Kansas City: Sheed Andrews and McMeel, 1976.

Knight, Frank H. "'What is Truth' in Economics." In *On the History and Method of Economics*, edited by William L. Letwin and Alexander J. Morin, pp. 151–178. Chicago: University of Chicago Press, 1956.

Leoni, Bruno, and Frola, Eugenio. "On Mathematical Thinking in Economics." *Journal of Libertarian Studies* 1:101–109.

McKenzie, Richard E. "The Neoclassicalists vs. the Austrians: A Partial Reconciliation of Competing Worldviews." *Southern Economic Journal*, vol. 47, no. 1 (July 1980), pp. 1–13.

Mises, Ludwig von. *Epistemological Problems of Economics*. Princeton, N.J.: Van Nostrand, 1960.

———. *Human Action: A Treatise on Economics*. New Haven: Yale University Press, 1963.

———. *The Ultimate Foundation of Economic Science*. Kansas City: Sheed Andrews and McMeel, 1978.

Rothbard, Murray N. "In Defense of 'Extreme Apriorism.'" *Southern Economic Journal* 23 (1957):314–20.

———. *Man, Economy, and State: A Treatise on Economic Principles*. 2d ed., pp. 1–66. Kansas City: Sheed Andrews and McMeel, 1970.

———. *Toward a Reconstruction of Utility and Welfare Economics*. New York: Center for Libertarian Studies, 1976.

Schoeck, H., and Wiggins, J. W., eds. *Relativism and the Study of Man*. Princeton, N.J.: Van Nostrand, 1961.

Watkins, J. W. N. "Types of Historical Explanation," "Ideal Historical Explanation in the Social Sciences," "Methodological Individualism: A Reply." In *Modes of Individualism and Collectivism*, edited by John O'Neill. New York: St. Martin's Press, 1973.

White, Lawrence H. *Methodology of the Austrian School*. New York: Center for Libertarian Studies, 1977.

Wild, John, and Cobitz, J. L. "On the Distinction Between the Analytic and Synthetic." *Philosophy and Phenomenological Research* 8 (June 1948):651–67.

Wong, Hao. "Notes on the Analytic-Synthetic Distinction." *Theoria* 21 (1955):158.

ABOUT THE AUTHOR

James B. Ramsey was born in 1937 in the United States, but brought up in England and educated at Chigwell School in Essex. After serving in the Royal Signals in Cyprus, 1956–58, he emigrated to Canada and studied at the University of British Columbia, gaining a B.A. in economics in 1963, and an M.A. (Econ.) (1964) and Ph.D. (Econ.) (1968) at the University of Wisconsin, Madison.

From 1963 to 1966 he was an economic consultant to the Department of Northern Affairs and National Resources of the Canadian government. From 1966 he was successively assistant professor, associate professor, and, from 1972 to 1976, professor of economics at Michigan State University. From 1971 to 1973 he was also professor of econometrics and social statistics at the University of Birmingham (England). He is currently professor of economics at New York University.

Professor Ramsey's numerous publications cover a wide variety of topics in economic theory, econometric theory and methodology, and in applied economics. While he is predominantly concerned with developing theory, his concern is not for its own sake, nor for the pleasure of indulging in mathematical games, but as a tool to be used in understanding the world. He is best known for his work in testing economic theory and using it in real life.

The Cato Papers

Reprinted by the Cato Institute, the Papers in this series have been selected for their singular contributions to such fields as economics, history, philosophy, and public policy.

Copies of the *Cato Papers* may be ordered from the Publications Department, Cato Institute, 747 Front Street, San Francisco, California 94111.